DASA MAHAV

The Ten Great Tantric Wisdom Goddesses

VINITA RASHINKAR

Illustrations: Manoj Raj, Incredible Design

Cover design: Velu T, Bluebrick

Author photo: Konen Raza, Qatar

INDIA · SINGAPORE · MALAYSIA

Dedication

I humbly dedicate this book to our honourable Prime Minister, Sri Narendra Modiji, the embodiment of unwavering strength and unparalleled wisdom, whose resolute commitment to upholding the eternal flame of Sanatana Dharma has kindled the depths of our souls, igniting a fervent passion for our glorious heritage. In his sacred presence, we stand united, adorned with the pride that envelops our sacred land, Bharat.

Jai Hind!

SRI MATRYE NAMAH

For Puja, Amit and Snowy

Contents

Dasa Mahavidya

Blurb

In the mystical realms of the ancient Tantra tradition, a hidden path beckons, veiled in unparalleled mystery and brimming with extraordinary power—the path of the Dasa Mahavidya, the Ten Great Tantric Wisdom Goddesses. Plunge into the sacred depths of the Dasa Mahavidya, as the wisdom of ages past fuses seamlessly with contemporary insight. Each chapter unveils magnificent tales, revealing the extraordinary essence of a different goddess. Witness the awe-inspiring might of Kali, the relentless destroyer of illusions, as she wields her cosmic blade to sever the bonds of ignorance. Encounter Lalita Tripura Sundari, the enchantress supreme, whose grace can manifest unimaginable miracles. And bask in the benevolence of Kamalatmika, the radiant bestower of abundance and prosperity, whose tender touch can transform lives. Guided by the hallowed whispers of ancient sages and the ethereal echoes of age-old tantric rituals, immerse in the profound teachings that stir dormant energies, unleashing the boundless power of divine feminine energy. Unveil the secrets of tantra, mantra, and yantra of these ten goddesses—the sacred triad that unlocks the portals to transcendent realms. This book takes you on an expedition through dimensions where darkness and light engage in a mesmerizing dance, where the very limits of human perception crumble like sandcastles, and where the sovereignty of divine femininity reigns supreme. In the hallowed domains of tantric wisdom, the goddesses stand ready to anoint the path with their benevolent blessings, illuminating the path with their divine radiance.

Author bio:

Vinita Rashinkar is a health and wellness expert, writer, speaker, spiritual counsellor and healer. She derives satisfaction from helping people find happiness and in aiding them lead a healthy and meaningful life. She has studied the principles of Ayurveda, yoga, meditation, chanting, chakras and stress management under various masters for the past 20 years. She has a Master's degree in English Literature.

Vinita is the Founder and Managing Director of Amara Vedic Wellness GmbH, a Dusseldorf-based company which aims at bringing hidden aspects of Vedic knowledge to the common man. Vinita has been a regular contributor to popular publications and portals, writing on subjects of health and lifestyle. She is also the Founder-Director of Bluebrick PR, a specialised international tourism marketing company.

Vinita has been featured in various Indian and international publications such as Femina, Outlook, Asiaspa, Finest Finance and Vogue. She is currently working with a major TV channel to provide health and wellness content.

For more information please see www.vinitarashinkar.in

Preface

Adi shakti, adi shakti, adi shakti, namo namo
Sarva shakti, sarva shakti, sarva shakti, namo namo
Pritam bhagavati, pritam bhagavati, pritam bhagavati, namo namo
Kundalini mata shakti, mata shakti, namo namo

Primal shakti, I bow to thee
All-encompassing shakti, I bow to thee
That through which divine creates, I bow to thee
Creative power of the Kundalini, mother of all mother power, I bow to thee

Goddesses play a pivotal role in the study and practice of Hinduism, particularly within the intricate realms of Tantric philosophy. They are regarded as central to understanding the nature of reality, often even more so than their male counterparts. Within the vast pantheon of female deities, there exists a profound and awe-inspiring tradition known as the Dasa Mahavidya. The term Dasa Mahavidya translates to "ten great knowledge systems" or "ten supreme wisdoms," denoting the philosophical heights of Vedic philosophy and the esoteric teachings of Hinduism. These ten great goddesses, revered as the embodiments of divine wisdom and cosmic power, are shrouded in ancient mythologies and revered scriptures. They offer deep insights into the nature of existence, the dynamics of creation and destruction, and the path to spiritual liberation.

It is with utmost reverence that I present this book, a comprehensive guide to the Dasa Mahavidya, crafted with the intent to provide readers with an understanding of their purpose and goals. This book is an effort to explore the intricate relationship between Dasa Mahavidya and Time (Kala in Vedic literature), Tantra, and Sri Vidya while delving into their association with Shakti. By examining their unique attributes, interconnections, and transformative practices linked to each Mahavidya, I hope to provide readers with an understanding of the divine presence of Shakti within the realm of Mahavidya.

Through this exploration, I hope to gain a deeper understanding, for myself as well as for my readers, of the Mahavidya's role in the expansive realm of the growth of the Shakti movement in Hindu theology and its profound impact on Tantric practices. I endeavour to unravel the mysteries surrounding the Dasa Mahavidya, peering into the depths of their symbolism, significance, and spiritual teachings. Drawing from ancient texts and esoteric knowledge, I explore their individual attributes and the profound lessons they impart. By diving into their mythologies and practices, I seek to unlock the transformative power of the Mahavidya, enabling us to navigate the complexities of existence and discover our own divine potential.

Revered as the primordial cosmic energy, Shakti stands as the paramount force that pervades all creation. Shakti is the dynamic power that fuels the universe, the pulsating life force that infuses every atom and molecule. It is within this sacred framework that the Dasa Mahavidya unfolds their divine manifestations, serving as embodiments of Shakti's infinite potential and boundless grace.

Shakti, depicted as the divine feminine principle, represents the creative and transformative energy that animates existence itself. In the context of the Dasa Mahavidya, Shakti assumes various forms, each imbued with distinct qualities, attributes, and cosmic responsibilities. These ten goddesses embody the multifaceted aspects of Shakti, providing a comprehensive outline for understanding and harnessing her divine power.

Each Mahavidya encompasses a unique aspect of Shakti's divine energy, representing different facets of life's journey, cosmic forces, and human experiences. From the fierce and transformative Kali, who symbolizes destruction and liberation, to the enchanting Kamalatmika, the epitome of grace and abundance, these goddesses guide us through the intricate journey of human existence, inviting us to explore the depths of our own consciousness and awaken to our true potential.

The Dasa Mahavidya extends far beyond the realm of myth and ritual. It holds profound implications for personal transformation, spiritual evolution, and the attainment of enlightenment. By immersing ourselves in the wisdom of these goddesses, we gain insights into the complexities of our own nature, unravelling the layers of conditioning and ego, and discovering the divine spark within.

The teachings of the Dasa Mahavidya emphasize the integration of Shakti's energy into our daily lives, fostering a harmonious balance between the material and spiritual realms. Through practices such as mantra, meditation, and ritual, we can tap into the transformative power of Shakti, aligning our individual consciousness with the cosmic energy that permeates the universe.

As we traverse the realms of Kali, Tara, Lalita Tripura Sundari, Bhuvaneshwari, Bhairavi, Chhinnamasta, Dhumavati, Bagalamukhi, Matangi, and Kamalatmika, we come face to face with the multifaceted nature of the divine feminine and the transformative power it holds.

Each goddess, with her unique essence and purpose, serves as a mirror, reflecting different aspects of our own inner selves and guiding us towards self-realization and spiritual growth, empowering us to embrace their teachings and embody their divine qualities in our own lives. I hope this exploration awakens a deep reverence within us for the divine feminine and her transformative energy. I pray that it inspires us to honour the sacredness within ourselves and all of creation.

With deep gratitude and reverence for the wisdom of the ages, I humbly offer this book as an offering to the ever-flowing river of knowledge, with the hope that it may contribute to the spiritual growth and well-being of all those who seek to unravel the mysteries of the Dasa Mahavidya.

Namaste

Vinita Rashinkar

Introduction

Shiva shaktya yukto yadi bhavati shaktah prabhavitum
na chadevam devo na khalu kushalah spanditumapi
Atastvam aradhyam hariharavirin chadi bhirapi
pranantum stotum va kathamakrta punyah prabhavati

Shiva becomes capable of creating the universe only when united
with Shakti
Otherwise he is incapable of even a stir
How then could one, who has not acquired merit in this and
previous births Worship or at least praise you, O divine mother,
who is adored even by Vishnu, Shiva, Brahma and others?

Shloka 1, Saundarya Lahiri by Adi Shankaracharya

In the Tantric tradition, the universe is alive and brimming with joy and bliss. All manifestations are seen as an interplay between Shiva, who symbolizes pure consciousness, the unchanging, unlimited masculine principle, and Shakti, representing the activating energy, the Mother, the feminine principle. Shiva and Shakti are merely manifestations of the Brahman, but it is only when Shiva and Shakti combine that creation can occur. Shiva is referred to as the Supreme Being or the ultimate reality, representing the transcendent aspect of divinity. He is associated with stillness and meditation and is seen as the ultimate source of all creation. He is also known as the destroyer, as he symbolizes the dissolution of the universe to make way for new creation. Shakti is the source of all the principles and energies of the universe. The immense diversity of the manifestations of Shakti is seen in nature - in cosmic bodies, forces, nature, all of life's creations, and human beings. These are all expressions of Shakti's vidya. Therefore, the symbols of these energies and their expressions are regarded with awe, wonder, and reverence and are known as "Maha" (great) Vidya.

The growth of goddesses can be observed through the evolution of Hinduism over time. In the traditional androcentric denominations of Hinduism, goddesses were relegated to the role of consorts and auxiliary deities to the more eminent male deities such as Shiva, Vishnu, and Brahma. The Vedas contain references to only a few goddesses, such as Ushas, the goddess of dawn; Aditi, hailed as the mother of gods such as Indra, Mitra, Varuna, and the Adityas, Prithvi, the "Earth" goddess, seen as the embodiment of the earth element; and Vac, also known as Saraswati, representing the power of speech and communication.

The prominence of goddesses increased significantly in post Vedic period. The Puranas, a genre of Hindu scriptures composed between the third and sixteenth centuries, played a crucial role in elevating the status of goddesses. In the Puranas, we see for the first time, texts dedicated with entire sections to various goddesses and their mythologies. Goddesses like Durga, Lakshmi, Saraswati, and Kali gained prominence through Puranic literature. The Bhakti movement, which emerged in medieval India, emphasized personal devotion and the worship of deities. During this period, many poets and saints composed devotional hymns and songs dedicated to goddesses. This led to a surge in the popularity of goddess worship among the masses. The Shakta tradition celebrates the goddess as the supreme power, and its practices involve rituals, meditation, and the chanting of goddess mantras. This tradition has significantly contributed to the growth of goddess worship in Hinduism.

In Shaktism, goddesses are revered and hold preeminent roles. Shakti is believed to manifest in various forms, with the following being particularly significant:

- Tridevi

- Navadurga

- Dasa Mahavidya

The term "Tridevi" refers to the three primary goddesses in Shaktism who represent the cosmic forces of creation, preservation, and destruction.

- Durga symbolizes the power of divine femininity and is renowned for her fierce form. She is depicted as riding a lion or tiger, and she wields various weapons in her multiple arms. Durga is believed to protect the universe from evil forces and is worshipped as the embodiment of courage and righteousness.

- Lakshmi represents wealth, abundance, and prosperity. She is associated with good fortune, fertility, and material well-being. Lakshmi is depicted as a beautiful goddess seated on a lotus flower, often accompanied by elephants. She is worshipped to attain wealth and spiritual prosperity.

- Saraswati is the deity of knowledge, arts, music, and wisdom. She is revered as the source of intellect and creativity. Saraswati is depicted playing a veena (a musical instrument) and is associated with the purity of thought and expression. She is worshipped by students, artists, and scholars to seek wisdom and artistic inspiration.

The Tridevi represents the three fundamental aspects of existence and embodies the cosmic powers of creation, preservation, and dissolution.

Durga then manifests in nine material forms as Navadurga to operate the nine planets in order to maintain cosmic balance.

Each form represents a different aspect and power of the goddess and comes into prominence during the Navratri festival. In certain regions and traditions, there are four Navratris celebrated in a year. These Navratris are observed during different seasons and have their own unique significance.

- Vasanta Navratri, also known as Chaitra Navratri, is observed during the Hindu month of Chaitra (March-April). It is celebrated to welcome the spring season and marks the beginning of the traditional Hindu New Year. In some regions, the ninth day is celebrated as Ram Navami, the birth anniversary of Lord Rama.

- Gupt Navratri, also called Ashadha Navratri, takes place during the Hindu month of Ashadha (June-July). This Navratri is not as widely celebrated as the other three Navratris. It is considered a period of introspection and spiritual sadhana (practice). Devotees engage in fasting, prayers, and meditation during this time to seek spiritual growth.

- Sharad Navratri, also known as Maha Navratri, is the most popular and widely celebrated Navratri festival. It occurs during the Hindu month of Ashwin (September-October). Sharad Navratri is marked by elaborate rituals, fasting, and vibrant celebrations across India. It culminates on the tenth day with Vijayadashami, or Dussehra, symbolizing the victory of good over evil.

- Magha Navratri, also referred to as Magh Gupt Navratri, is observed during the Hindu month of Magha (January-February). It is considered a more subdued and secretive Navratri and is not as widely celebrated as the other Navratris. Devotees perform spiritual practices, engage in meditation, and offer prayers during this period.

While Sharad Navratri is the most prominent and popularly celebrated Navratri, the other three Navratris also hold significance as they provide opportunities to deepen the spiritual connection, seek blessings, and engage in devotional practices throughout the year.

Each Navadurga is worshipped on a specific day of Navratri:

1. Shailaputri is associated with the energy of mountains. She is depicted as a young girl holding a trident and riding a bull. She signifies the start of the Navadurga sequence and represents the pure and innocent form of the goddess.

2. Brahmacharini symbolizes the unmarried and ascetic aspects of the goddess. She is depicted as walking barefoot, holding a rosary and a water pot. Brahmacharini represents self-control, knowledge, and the pursuit of truth.

3. Chandraghanta is known for the half-moon-shaped bell (ghanta) on her forehead. She is depicted with a fierce expression, riding a tiger. She represents bravery and courage and is worshipped for protection and strength.

4. Kushmanda is believed to have created the universe with her cosmic smile. She is depicted with eight arms and rides a lion or tiger. She represents cosmic energy and bestows health, strength, and prosperity.

5. Skandamata is depicted as holding her son, Lord Skanda (Kartikeya), on her lap. She symbolizes motherhood and nurturing love. She blesses her devotees with wisdom and guidance.

6. Katyayani is known for her fierce and warrior-like appearance. She is depicted with four arms, holding a sword and a lotus. She represents courage and helps devotees overcome obstacles and negative energies.

7. Kalaratri is a fierce and dark goddess. She is depicted with a terrifying appearance, wild hair, and a necklace of skulls. She symbolizes the dark and destructive aspects of life and destroys ignorance and removes fear.

8. Mahagauri represents purity and tranquillity. She is depicted as a radiant and compassionate goddess, dressed in white garments. She blesses devotees with peace, wisdom, and spiritual growth.

9. Siddhidatri represents the bestower of supernatural powers and spiritual achievements. She is depicted with four arms and is worshipped for her divine grace and blessings.

The worship of Navadurga during Navratri is considered a powerful way to connect with the divine feminine energy and seek blessings for various aspects of life, such as strength, knowledge, protection, and spiritual growth. By worshipping Navadurga, devotees invoke the collective power of the goddess and experience her divine grace in their lives.

As Vidya Shakti, Durga manifests as ten types of eternal knowledge, representing various aspects of power and wisdom. The Mahavidya tradition believes that "the one Truth is sensed in ten different facets; the Divine Mother is adored and approached as ten cosmic personalities. Even though Her Vidya is infinite and all-pervasive, it is classified into ten Mahavidya to simplify the sadhana for the seeker.

The ten Mahavidya are:

1. Kali: Symbolizing destruction, time, and ultimate reality

2. Tara: Associated with compassion, healing, and protection

3. Lalita Tripura Sundari: Representing beauty, divine love, and harmony

4. Bhuvaneshwari: Symbolizing the universe and cosmic existence

5. Chhinnamasta: Associated with self-sacrifice and liberation

6. Bhairavi: Representing fierce power and divine wrath

7. Dhumavati: Symbolizing widows, inauspiciousness, and detachment

8. Bagalamukhi: Associated with protection and stopping negativity

9. Matangi: Representing speech and impurity

10. Kamala: Symbolizing wealth, abundance, and spiritual growth

The history and origin of the Dasa Mahavidya are shrouded in mystery and debate, as there is no definitive historical record of their creation. However, there are several theories about the origins of the Mahavidya based on religious texts, mythology, and historical accounts.

One theory is that the Mahavidya have their roots in the ancient Vedic tradition, which predates the development of Hinduism as we know it today. In the Vedic tradition, there were ten goddesses known as the Dasharupa, or the ten forms of the goddess. Some scholars believe that some of the Mahavidya may have evolved from these ten goddesses, with additional deities being added over time.

Another theory is that the Mahavidya emerged as a distinct group of goddesses within the Hindu pantheon during the medieval period, around the 7th to 13th centuries CE. During this period, there was a resurgence of the worship of the goddess in India, and the Mahavidya may have been created as part of this movement.

The Guhyati Guyhatantra associates the Mahavidya with the Dashavatara, the ten avatars of Vishnu, and states that the Mahavidya are the source from which the avatars of Vishnu arise.

The Dashavatara refers to the ten primary incarnations of Lord Vishnu, the preserver and protector of the universe, as described in Hindu mythology. The Dashavatara includes incarnations such as Matsya (the fish), Kurma (the tortoise), Varaha (the boar), Narasimha (the half-lion, half-human), Vamana (the dwarf), Parashurama (the warrior-sage), Rama (the prince of Ayodhya), Krishna (the divine cowherd), Buddha (the enlightened one), and Kalki (the future incarnation).

In the Todalatantra, chapter ten, Devi asks Shiva to reveal to her which avatar is associated with each Mahavidya. Shiva is said to have replied: "Tara Devi is the blue form, Bagala is the tortoise incarnation, Dhumavati is the boar; Chhinnamasta is Narasimha; Bhuvaneshwari is Vamana; Matangi is the Buddha form; Tripura Sundari is Jamadagni; Bhairavi is Balabhadra; Kamalatmika is Matsya; and Bhagavati Kali is Krishna murti."

Association between the Mahavidya and the Dashavatara	
Mahavidya	**Dashavatara**
Kali	Krishna
Tara	Rama
Lalita Tripurasundari	Kalki
Bhuvaneshwari	Varaha
Bhairavi	Narasimha
Chhinnamasta	Parashurama
Dhumavati	Vamana
Bagalamukhi	Kurma
Matangi	Buddha
Kamalatmika	Matsya

The development of the Mahavidya represents an important turning point in the history of Shaktism as it marks the rise of the Bhakti aspect, which reached its zenith in 1700 CE. It first sprung forth in the post-Puranic age, around the sixth century C.E., as a new theistic movement in which the supreme being was envisioned as female, a fact epitomized by texts like the Devi-Bhagavata Purana, especially its last nine chapters of the seventh skandha, which are known as the Devi Gita and soon became central texts of Shaktism.

The growth of the Mahavidya brought about several changes in Shaktism, including a new emphasis on the Divine Feminine. By representing a diverse group of goddesses, with different origins, mythologies, and iconography, a new inclusivity was introduced, which reflected a broader acceptance of different regional and local traditions within Shaktism. Each of the Mahavidya has her own unique characteristics, qualities, and iconography. This emphasis on individuality reflects a more nuanced understanding of the divine and allows for a greater personal connection to the goddesses.

Devadutta Kali writes in The Power of Consciousness that "the highest spiritual truth is that reality is One. When personified as the Divine Mother, that reality expresses itself in countless ways. The ten Mahavidya, or Wisdom Goddesses, represent distinct aspects of divinity that guide the spiritual seeker toward liberation. These forms can be approached in a spirit of reverence, love, and increasing intimacy for the devotionally minded seeker. For a knowledge-oriented seeker, these same forms can represent various states of inner awakening along the path to enlightenment."

The Origin Story of Dasa Mahavidya

A story from the Shakta-Maha-Bhagavata-Purana narrates the origin of the Dasa Mahavidya. Sati, daughter of Daksha Prajapathi, is madly in love with Shiva and marries him against her father's wishes. Daksha, an arrogant and angry ruler, decides to conduct a yagna, to which he invites all the gods except his son-in-law Shiva. This angers Sati greatly, as she sees it as an insult to her husband and makes up her mind to attend the yagna. She goes to Shiva to seek his permission, but he refuses to let her go, stating that even if she went, the fruit of the yagna would remain inauspicious.

Sati gets very angry with Shiva for what she perceives as insulting her intelligence and wishes to show him her power. Shiva is afraid and tries to escape her wrath. She appears in ten different forms, guarding each of the ten directions. These ten forms jointly subdue Shiva's resistance, and Sati goes on to attend the sacrificial ritual. Upon seeing ten powerful Shaktis surrounding him, Shiva asks:

"Who are you all? Where is my Sati?"

Bhairavi, one of the forms Sati has taken, replies:

"I am your Sati, the furious images found around you are my ten different incarnations, do not be afraid of them."

The Chamunda Tantra lists these ten forms as Dasa Mahavidya.

> Kali Tara Mahavidya Shodashi Bhuvaneshwari
> Bhairavi Chinnamasta cha vidya Dhumavati tatha
> Bagala sidhdhavidya cha Matangi Kamalatmika
> Iti Dasa Mahavidya sidhdhavidya prakirtita

Each of these forms has been given a name, a story, unique physical attributes, and personality traits. Their characteristic sadhana covers three fundamental points:

1. Devotion to the image of the deity

2. Meditation on the yantra

3. Chanting the mantra

Each of the Mahavidya is also associated with specific planets, elements, and chakras, which are believed to be influenced by their energy.

Ugra and Soumya Forms

According to Advaita Vedanta, the human mind is conditioned and operates within the realm of duality, concepts, and limitations. It relies on sensory perception and conceptual understanding to grasp the world around it. The formless, infinite nature of divine reality transcends the boundaries of the human mind and cannot be directly comprehended through ordinary means.

Recognizing the limitations of the human mind, Advaita schools emphasize the use of a concrete form, such as the various devatas, as a means to connect with and understand the divine. A form serves as a focal point for devotion and meditation, providing a tangible representation of the formless divine reality. It acts as a bridge between limited human perception and the infinite divine.

The use of devatas in worship and meditation helps the mind to concentrate and direct one's devotion towards the divine. By providing a specific form to focus on, the mind is guided away from distractions and worldly attachments, facilitating a deeper connection with the divine presence. The devata becomes a symbol of reverence and love, aiding in the development of devotion and surrender. While a devata is a temporary form, it serves as a stepping stone towards transcending the limitations of form and perceiving formless reality. Through sustained practice and spiritual discipline, the devotee gradually realizes that the devata is not merely an external object, but a reflection of the divine presence within himself.

The use of different devatas with their unique name-form and characteristics is a skillful way to help the mind transcend its limitations and recognize the formless reality that underlies all manifestations. These representations are not to be understood literally but rather as metaphors for deeper philosophical concepts. Deities are depicted with different qualities and can largely be divided into Soumya (gentle), Ugra (fierce) and Soumya-Ugra (gentle/ fierce based on situation) forms, representing different aspects of the divine energy and serving as complementary expressions of the multifaceted nature of divinity and the complexity of human existence.

- Ganapathi, Lakshmi, Lalita, and Krishna are examples of Soumya devatas

- Kali, Rudra, Mrityunjaya and Narasimha are Ugra devatas

- Hanuman, Lakshmi Narasimha and Tara are Soumya/ Ugra devatas

Advaita Vedanta recognizes that individuals have unique temperaments, preferences, and spiritual needs. Therefore, the choice of a specific devata may vary among practitioners. Some may be drawn to deities like Shiva, Vishnu, or Devi, while others may choose a personal deity based on their cultural or familial tradition. This personalized approach allows individuals to connect with the divine in a way that resonates with their own spiritual journey. Aditi Banerjee says in an article in Swarajya magazine that Hinduism allows its followers to choose a form that is most suitable for their spiritual evolution in accordance with their personality and psychological needs. She adds, "The Hindu way promotes diversity and inclusiveness; heterogeneity of worship promotes heterogeneity of mind and philosophy. It teaches us to see beauty and divinity in all forms, even those that may not readily appear beautiful or divine to us. We must not shy away from the fierce, from what appears shocking, ugly, or even frightening. We must learn to see beauty beyond its superficial appearance. It is a mistake to equate spirituality only with sattva. As Sri Krishna instructs Arjuna in the Bhagavad Gita,

Traigunya vishaya veda nistraigunyo bhava arjuna

The Vedas deal with the three attributes of nature (tamas, rajas, and sattva); be thou above these three attributes, O Arjuna! (Bhagavad Gita, 2:45)

In other words, one should not become too attached to the quality of sattva—all three modes of nature are to be transcended. All forms provide devotees with diverse perspectives and avenues for spiritual growth, allowing individuals to connect with the divine in a way that resonates with their unique temperament and spiritual aspirations."

Krishna explains in the Bhagavad Gita that when people's desires control them, their innate 'swabhava' compels each of them to seek divine assistance. The Sanskrit word bhava means habitual or emotional tendencies. "Whatever deity a jiva wants to worship, I will strengthen his devotion", Krishna says, describing Brahman as the antaryami in all the forms of deities that people worship. It is He who grants their desires. He does so to strengthen their devotion.

In his book Mahanirvana Tantra, Sir John Woodroffe writes that "the form of worship and sadhana is based on the individual temperament of the sadhaka. They worship the various deities and pray to them to grant them their wishes as well as for guidance to enable them to cross the vicissitudes of life."

The gentle and benevolent Soumya forms, emanate a peaceful, serene, and compassionate energy. These deities embody qualities such as love, nurturing, wisdom, and grace. The Soumya forms are associated with wisdom, knowledge, and enlightenment and are seen as divine intelligence that guides and illuminates the path of spiritual seekers. Deities such as Saraswati (the goddess of knowledge) represent the power of intellect, learning, and creative inspiration. Devotees seek their blessings to attain wisdom, creativity, and intellectual prowess.

The tranquil and serene countenances of Soumya forms inspire a sense of peace and tranquillity in the hearts of their devotees. Deities such as Lakshmi (goddess of wealth and prosperity) represent abundance and bring auspiciousness, harmony, and prosperity.

The Soumya forms exemplify qualities such as forgiveness, and mercy. Goddesses such as Parvati and Annapurna (goddess of food and nourishment), shower their devotees with divine understanding, and forgiveness. Devotees seek their blessings to cultivate these qualities within themselves and to overcome difficulties with grace and empathy.

These gentle forms highlight the underlying unity and harmony in the diverse expressions, especially of the divine feminine. They represent the unifying force that connects all beings and fosters harmony in the universe. Goddesses, such as Radha (consort of Krishna) and Sita (the consort of Rama), symbolize the divine love that unites the individual soul with the universal consciousness.

The worship of goddesses in their Soumya forms provides devotees with a sense of solace and inspiration. It reminds individuals of the qualities they can cultivate within themselves, such as love, compassion, wisdom, and serenity. The Soumya forms of goddesses serve as role models, guiding devotees towards a path of self-realization, inner peace, and harmonious existence. Soumya forms also provide a strong counterbalance to the fierce depictions of deities and showcase the harmony and diversity within the Hindu pantheon.

Jessica Frazier writes in 'A Little History of the Fierce Goddess': "Fierce goddesses exist across the world, but Hinduism is unusually rich in them. There is fanged Bhadrakali, skeletal Chamunda, lion-headed Narasimhi, the goddess Chhinnamasta, who decapitates herself atop a copulating couple, and haggard Dhumavati, the goddess of quarrels, solitude, hunger, and age. These female deities present a riddle for anyone who expects gods to be pleasant. Sociologically, such deities are an anomaly. Early Indo-Aryan religions often followed an 'exchange' model: each deity offered some boon in return for our worship. This principle is easy to see in thunderbolt-wielding father gods like Jehovah, Zeus, and Indra, who give protection, or sun gods like Ra, Ahura Mazda, or Surya, who shed their grace from above each day.

Dark goddesses can fit into this pattern too. One Vedic hymn pleads with the goddess of chaos, Nirrti, to stay distant, revealing a 'please keep away' style of worship. Sitala, the smallpox goddess, arrives with the spirit of fever but happily departs if propitiated in the right way. When she leaves, the healthy devotee then praises her as Bhagavati or Mangala - the auspicious one."

The depiction of deities as fierce and powerful beings is intended to convey profound aspects of divine energy and reflect the complex nature of existence. The fierce forms symbolize the destruction of ignorance, ego, and the forces of darkness. They embody the divine power that annihilates negative qualities and obstacles on the spiritual path. By depicting deities who are angry, bloodthirsty, war-mongering, and violent, the strength and determination required to overcome internal and external challenges are highlighted. The fierce forms, especially of the goddesses, represent the protective and nurturing aspects of the divine feminine. Just as a mother fiercely protects her child from harm, these goddesses embody the fierce determination to safeguard devotees from evil and injustice. Their ferocity is an expression of their boundless love and dedication to preserving righteousness and justice in the world.

The fierce depictions of goddesses also prompt us to accept and embrace the paradoxical nature of existence. They remind us that divinity encompasses both creation and destruction, gentleness and fierceness, beauty and wrath. By embracing these contradictions, devotees are encouraged to transcend dualistic thinking and perceive the underlying unity in all aspects of life. The fierce forms symbolize the transformative power of divine energy by representing the intensity required to break through limitations, attachments, and illusions on the path to self-realization. Through their fierce appearances, goddesses inspire devotees to confront and transcend fear, confront their own inner challenges, transform negative tendencies, and awaken their dormant spiritual potential.

The fierce depictions of goddesses should not be interpreted as encouraging violence or aggression. Rather, they serve as powerful metaphors and symbols that are a reminder of the multifaceted nature of divinity. The darker, deeper aspects of our nature are not to be shunned or suppressed. These recesses of our personalities are storehouses of immense amounts of energy that can be conducive and important to our spiritual and psychological development when appropriately channelled. Our personalities can benefit from what the Ugra Devatas and their worship represent.

In the Mahavidya, the ten Goddesses can be categorized as below:

Soumya

Lalita Tripurasundari

Bhuvaneshwari

Matangi

Kamalatmika

Ugra

Kali

Chhinna Masta

Dhumavati

Bagalamukhi

Soumy-ugra

Tara

Bhairavi

Ishta devata

Every family that follows Sanatana Dharma identifies with three principal deities: kula devata, grama devata, and ishta devata. The first two are determined by birth, and the third is based on the individual's personal choice. Kula Devata, or the "clan deity," is a time-honoured family deity worshipped by generations. By custom, the family deity never changes for the paternal hierarchy of family members. However, after marriage, a woman starts worshiping the kula devata of her husband. There are several references to the kula devata in the Puranas, with a note that pooja is to be offered to the clan deity before auspicious events, such as marriage or the birth of a child. It is believed that rituals done at a kuladeva or kuladevi temple benefit all those genetically connected with the one performing the ritual.

A grama devata, or village deity, is the tutelary deity of a given locality, primarily worshipped in the villages. Of diverse origins, grama devatas are regarded as protecting the inhabitants of their villages from bandits, epidemics, and natural disasters when propitiated, failing which they are believed to cause these afflictions. A grama devata is typically female in South India. In this region, a village goddess, acting as a fertility figure, is enshrined, and a guardian of the village is situated at the village boundary.

An ishta devata is the personal deity with whom a devotee feels the greatest affinity, or the god whose distinct blessings are most needed by the worshiper to help with a specific problem or desire. The essence of the ishta devata relationship is 'smarana', or constant, continuous remembrance. Remembering the deity and internally building a relationship with them is considered essential to the sadhana. Through smarana and various spiritual practices aimed at the ishta devata, we come to the point where we accept the ishta devata as a force that guides us through life, helps us live a fulfilling and spiritually protected life, and then finally guides our soul to its real home - moksha.

If you do not have a clear idea yet about a divine form or devata that you feel connected to in some way or feel the greatest affinity towards, then don't worry about it; your Ishta Devata will reveal himself or herself to you when the time is right for your sadhana to move to the next level.

Nithin Sridhar writes in a blog titled Ishta Devata: "Ishta devata can be considered in many senses as a unique contribution of Hinduism to the whole world, not only in terms of its theological and spiritual value but also in terms of promoting world harmony. In simple words, any person can connect with God or the Cosmos in the way he feels inclined to or is comfortable with."

Kavita Chinnaiyan writes: "The sadhana of the Mahavidya is not for the weak of heart. Each of these forms of Shakti represents an aspect of creation at both the macrocosmic and individual (ego) levels. While some worship the Mahavidya for power, dark magic, and siddhis, they get further enmeshed in her Maya and eventually succumb to her insurmountable power. It is not possible to win her grace through force or cunning. Only the willingness to give up the "I-ness" enables her grace to shine forth. This is the secret of tantra: one's spiritual progress is in direct proportion to the degree of surrender. Moreover, it is not necessary to worship all ten Mahavidya; each is a gateway to liberation, opening to the grace of all the others. After all, she is one, manifesting as all.

Shakti and Tantra

Hinduism holds three concepts at the very core of its essence: Brahman (the Absolute), Vedas (sacred knowledge), and Moksha (liberation from the never-ending cycle of death and rebirth). Brahman is the nature of truth, wisdom, and infinity, according to the Taittariya Upanishad "Satyam jnanam anantam brahman". It is above and beyond the human constructs of time, space, and matter. Brahman is derived from "brh," meaning "that which grows (brahati) or that which causes growth (brahmayati)". Brahman is often loosely translated as God, but a more profound study suggests a definite conception of the Absolute – it transcends all dualities and classifications. The Brahman is the Absolute Truth (param satya) and the omnipotent and animating life-principle (chit-atman).

The ultimate aim of a Hindu is to become one with the Brahman.

There are many paths to becoming one with the Brahman; knowledge, devotion, good deeds, and meditation are of primary importance. Still, there are no distinctions made between these paths, as they are bound to intersect and work in combination in the due process of living.

The first path to liberation is knowledge, which is contained in the Vedas, the oldest Hindu scriptures that contain information on all aspects of life. The word veda comes from "vid," meaning "to know," and it serves to manifest the language of Brahman to humanity. Tradition indicates that the Vedas were not composed by humans but were revealed to enlightened rishis or seers and passed down from generation to generation through oral tradition.

Vedic knowledge is said to be Shruti, that which has been heard (consisting of revelations); it is the unquestionable truth and can never change. Other forms of knowledge are "Smriti," the knowledge that is remembered (an outcome of the intellect) and can change over time.

The Vedas are not a mere collection of scriptures but a living, ever-expanding, dynamic communication between the Brahman and humanity using the subtle laws that govern the universe: sound, form, and colour. Humans can utilize the knowledge contained in the Vedas to lead them to moksha, which is liberation from suffering and the endless cycle of death and rebirth. It is the return to Brahman – the realization of the self as the Absolute.

Hindu dharma clearly states that liberation is not exclusively promised to one who embraces sanyasa. It is equally possible for a householder who aspires for material prosperity and enjoys a sensory life to seek moksha. In both cases, the pursuit of knowledge is the starting point of the journey. A sanyasi should pursue methods that would lead him to understand himself. In contrast, a householder should pursue learning, which becomes the basis of Dharma (moral duties), Artha (wealth creation), and Kama (sensual enjoyment).

While a sanyasi can seek his Brahma vidya through renunciation, asceticism, and meditation, a householder can begin his journey into the deepest point of his being through a study and practice of Tantra.

The Brihadaranyaka Upanishad, considered the crown jewel among all the Upanishads, carries the famous statement "Aham Brahmasmi" (I am Brahman). Hindu dharma's basic premise is that only one Supreme Being is given different names, forms, and specific qualities. This manifestation as various divine bodies helps establish a speedier connection between humans and the Divine as it reduces the Supreme Being to a more tangible, approachable, and relatable entity. Throughout the history of this ancient religion, many sects have formed as an outcome of devotion to one particular form or one specific philosophy. In general, Hinduism can be categorized into four major denominations:

- Vaishnavism: worship of Vishnu

- Shaivism: worship of Shiva

- Shaktism: worship of Mother Goddess, or Shakti

- Smarthaism: belief in the essential oneness of all gods; offers a personal choice to the worshipper to determine his own God.

All four denominations are united in a common purpose: to further the soul's unfoldment toward its divine destiny. Several concepts, such as accepting the Vedas as the ultimate authority and believing in the doctrines of karma, reincarnation, etc., are common to all. They differ primarily in terms of the deity worshipped by the particular sect as the Supreme Being and the traditions followed in offering worship to that deity. Each sect has its own temples, pilgrimage centres, sacred literature, and guru lineages.

Shaktas, as the practitioners of Shaktism are commonly known, conceive of the Goddess as a representation of the primordial energy and source of the cosmos. Shaktism is based on the Vedas, Upanishads, and Puranas that speak about this tradition's prevalence during different historical periods, beginning with early Vedic times, waxing and waning in its influence, and gaining maximum prominence during the Epic period. Shaktism is believed to have evolved out of a rebellion against the power that Brahmins exercised in society and a desire to return to the archetypal Mother Goddess concept that existed in prehistoric times. The essential propagators of Shaktism have been the practitioners of Advaita Vedanta such as the greatest Indian mystic saint, Adi Shankaracharya.

In Shaktism, the world is not approached as Maya or illusion. It is perceived as real and divine in all its aspects, even the ugly, gross, and unholy. Shakti evolves into thirty-six tattvas, or elements, to form the universe. Therefore, the universe and everything it contains are mere manifestations of Shakti. The Brihadaranyanka Upanishad references a spider spinning its web from its mouth and moving through its own creation of concentric circles, putting forth new threads and pulling back others while controlling all of its creation from one single point. This image conveys the essentially Vedic thought that all existence arises out of and eventually returns to one single principle. The human body is held sacred as it is the temple of our spiritual unfoldment.

Shaktism can be classified into Srikula, or the family of Lakshmi, and Kalikula, or the family of Kali. In both aspects, Shakti is worshipped by mantras, mudras, and yantras.

Tantra

One of Shaktism's most well-known sub-traditions is Tantra, which refers to techniques, practices, and rituals involving mantra, mudra, and yantra. In Hindu dharma, enlightenment is often seen as a process that takes several lifetimes. Tantra philosophy, however, suggests that enlightenment is possible in one lifetime. Tantra seeks to dissolve the separateness of the mundane from the spiritual. Every aspect of life is seen as a tool for spiritual growth. The body is seen as a living temple, and all its energies, positive or otherwise, are considered tools for spiritual progress and transformation. Tantra is profoundly devotional and highly ritualistic, but these rituals are a means to see and experience life and its energies as divine manifestations.

Leora Lightwoman explains how Tantra evolved into its present-day form in an article titled The History of Tantra:

"Tantra is not a religion, although Tantric symbology and practices have emerged throughout history in all religions and cultures. Tantric principles are inherent in mystical Judaism (Kabbalah), Christianity, and Sufism. Chinese Taoism is another strand of Tantra. Representations of the sacred union of masculine and feminine principles and the nonduality of this "sacred inner marriage" can be found as far back as 2000 BC in the Indus Valley civilization and the Egyptian Old Kingdom."

The origin and history of Tantra are shrouded in mystery and continue to be the subject of frequent discourse among theologians. Many scholars believe that Tantra began in the Indus Valley (current-day Pakistan and the north-western parts of India) between three thousand and five thousand years ago, when the Vedas were written. But Tantra did not come into common practice until the fourth century; around the same time, Patanjali's yoga philosophy began to take root and flourish.

The first Hindu and Buddhist Tantric texts can be traced back to 300–400 CE and were purposely obscure so that only initiates could understand them. Until then, Tantric teachings were closely guarded and transmitted orally from master to disciple only after long periods of preparation and purification. Tantra reached the height of its popularity in the 11th and 12th centuries, when it was practiced widely and openly in India.

Mathias Rose writes in The Origins of Tantra: "The teachings that began to spread throughout India had a powerful attraction to a populace that was increasingly well off and had a robust middle class. The prosperous middle class was, by and large, left out of the caste-conscious religions of Vedic origin and monastic male Buddhism. Moreover, unlike the well-established and increasingly scholarly traditions, these teachings were vibrant, immediate and taught that enlightenment was available right now. in this life. No reincarnation is needed. The Divine was seen not as an abstract and distant deity or collection of deities but as an all-pervasive presence that each of us is not just a part of but intriguingly the whole of. "

Renowned yoga scholar Georg Feuerstein believes that Tantra came about as a response to a period of spiritual decline, also known as Kali Yuga, or the Dark Age, that is still in progress today. He suggests that robust measures were needed to counteract the many obstacles (such as greed, dishonesty, physical and emotional illness, attachment to worldly things, and complacency) to spiritual liberation. He writes that "Tantra's comprehensive array of practices, which include asana and pranayama as well as mantra chanting, pujas (deity worship), kriyas (cleansing practices), mudras (hand gestures), and mandalas and yantras (circular or geometric patterns used to develop concentration), offered just that. Also, Tantra wasn't exclusively practiced by the noble Brahmin class. It gained power and momentum by being available to all types of people—men and women, Brahmins and lay people—who could all be initiated."

Significant debate surrounds the complex and, at times, controversial body of knowledge that constitutes Tantra. Until even a hundred years ago, not much was known to the world about the practices of Tantra, as most of the knowledge was passed down in India through the oral tradition from teacher to initiated disciple. In the Nath tradition, the origin of Tantra is ascribed to Dattatreya, who is said to be the author of the Jivanmukta Gita (Song of the Liberated Soul). Matsyendranath is the author of the Kaulajnana Nirnaya, a ninth century book that deals with several mystical subjects, including Tantra.

There are widely different Tantric texts, says meditation teacher Sally Kempton, "Different philosophical positions are taken by practitioners of Tantra. However, one core aspect of Tantric philosophy remains consistent: nondualism, or the idea that one's true essence (alternatively known as the transcendental Self, pure awareness, or the Divine) exists in every particle of the universe. In the non-dualist belief system, there is no separation between the material world and the spiritual realm. Although, as humans, we perceive duality all around us—good and bad, male and female, hot and cold—these are illusions created by the ego when, in fact, all opposites are contained in the same universal consciousness. For practitioners of Tantra, that means that everything you do and all that you sense, ranging from pain to pleasure and anything in between, is really a manifestation of the Divine and can be a means to bring you closer to your own divinity."

Tantra as a Path to Moksha

The Vedic knowledge "Shruti" is considered the highest form of knowledge. Shruti texts include two types of scriptures called Agama and Nigama. Agama is derived from the verb root "gama," which means "to go," and the preposition "a," which means "toward", and refers to scriptures as "that which have come down." Agama can therefore be understood as precepts and doctrines that have come down as tradition. Nigama, on the other hand, can be understood as a passage from the Vedas, a statement in the Vedic passage, a sacred tradition, or Vedic literature in general.

There are three types of Agama scriptures:

1. Vaishnava Agama, which is focused on Vishnu as the Supreme Being

2. Shaiva Agama, which sees Shiva as the Supreme Being

3. Shakta Agama, which regards Shakti as the Supreme Being

Tantra is seen as a subsystem of Shakta Agama. There is speculation among scholars about whether Tantra is a Vedic tradition. Pandit Vishwa, the founder of Vishwa Yoga, writes in his article on the difference between Vedas and Tantra: "In reality, the Vedic and Tantric traditions are both parts of one great system, even if there are a few differences in their approaches. The Vedic tradition is an Aryan one, while the Tantric practice is Dravidian in origin. The Vedic tradition is an earlier form of the tantric tradition. For example, the Atharva Veda is technically a tantric text. Therefore, it will be correct to assume that both the Tantra and the Vedas are important systems of Indian philosophy. Tantra glorifies individual power and practices, while the Vedas emphasize collective power and rituals. However, both share the common goal of self-realization."

Tantra represents the practical aspect of Vedic traditions. It is called a "Sadhana-shastra," which means it is practice-oriented as opposed to other philosophy-oriented traditions. Tantra accepts that the body exists with all its energies, good and evil; in the same way, the world exists with all its energies, good and bad. In this sense, Tantra is seen as a body-affirming and world-affirming spiritual tradition. This is in direct contrast to the classical view, which insists on renouncing worldly life to attain liberation. This aspect of Tantra allows householders to aspire for spiritual liberation while enjoying the sensory pleasures of life.

Leora Lightworker writes, "Tantra has been and still is practiced in three primary forms: the monastic tradition, the householder tradition, and by wandering yogis. Whereas Hinduism had many rules and laws, including strict caste divisions, Tantra was totally non-denominational and could be practiced by anyone, even in daily life. Thus, meditations on weaving, for example, could be practiced by weavers as they contemplated the interwoven and undifferentiated nature of existence. Kings and queens could practice meditation on eating, drinking, and lovemaking."

Tantra rests on three pillars:

1. The methodology, skills, and techniques

2. The mantras, which on a gross level, are unique sounds but on a deeper level are vehicles of consciousness. It is said that the world materialized through sound; therefore, sound acts as a link between the form and the formless.

3. The yantra, a geometric diagram used for rituals or worship and symbolically represents the entire universe

While Tantra, Mantra, and Yantra are the three pillars of the Tantra system, yoga is the practical application of Tantra.

Tantric Master Shri Aghorinath Ji says: "Tantra is different from other traditions because it takes the whole person with all their worldly desires into account. Other spiritual traditions ordinarily teach that desire for material pleasures, and spiritual aspirations are mutually exclusive, setting the stage for an endless internal struggle. Although most people are drawn into spiritual beliefs and practices, they have a natural urge to fulfill their desires. With no way to reconcile these two impulses, they fall prey to guilt and self-condemnation or become hypocritical. Tantra offers an alternative path."

There could not be a better way to explain Tantra. Shri Aghorinath has described in the above passage one of the most complex, grossly misunderstood, and misinterpreted terms of ancient Hindu traditions in the most straightforward manner. The word Tantra is sadly synonymous in the West with erotic sexual practices, while in India, it is most often labeled as occult and dark, sometimes known as "the left-hand path." Tantra suffers from its association with macabre Aghori traditions (eating or drinking from a skull, crematorium rituals, intoxication, sexual orgies).

The word itself is derived from two Sanskrit words, tan and tra: tan means to expand or spread and tra means instrument.

Tantra literally means a mechanism to expand consciousness. Some Vedic scholars also interpret the word tantra to mean "to weave," seeing the universe as a web in which everything is interconnected. Other scholars understand the word tantra to be a sly pun. Mathias Rose writes that one must first understand the word sutra to understand this pun. A core part of the prevailing religions (Buddhism, Jainism, and Vedic traditions) consisted of sutras, essential collections of compact principles. Etymologically, a sutra literally means thread; therefore, a sutra is a thread of thought or a particular line of thinking. If a sutra is a single thread of thought, Tantra is the whole system of thought. Therefore, the etymological essence of Tantra can be seen as the "next generation" advance in thinking about the sutras. Initially, sutras were a collection of aphorisms, while tantras were holistic spiritual teachings that could only be transmitted directly from teacher to student.

Tantra is generally classified into three primary schools, although there are many subdivisions within these:

- Kaula

- Mishra

- Samaya

Kaula Tantra is seen as the lower form of practice, and Samaya Tantra is the highest in the hierarchy of tantric practices. Kaula Tantra practice is focused on external rituals and processes. Mishra Tantra advocates a mixture of external rites and techniques combined with internal practices. Samaya Tantra describes an entirely internal process, a purely yogic practice with no use for external rituals.

The word kaula comes from the term "kula," meaning "family." This means two things: One, that people embracing family life can practice this path, and two, that everything in this universe is a part of one large family, much like in the concept of

Vasudaiva Kutumbakam expressed in later-day Vedic texts and philosophies.

Kaula practices consist mainly of worshipping external objects by way of rituals. These rituals include idols, mandalas, yantras, minerals, herbs, etc. The emphasis on this path is on devotion and faith, which are expressed through external worship. Many scholars point out that Kaula practices focus on the lowest three chakras, Muladhara, Swadisthana, and Manipura.

Within the Kaula Tantra, we see two types of paths: the left-handed path and the right-handed path, based on the practices that are followed. The left-hand path is known as Vamachara Marga, a non-conformist, non-orthodox path with no distinction between good and evil, pure and impure, clean and unclean. Sometimes it is seen as a path that uses means that go against the norms and ethics laid down by society. The Panchamakara ritual that some Tantra practitioners follow entails using taboo substances such as wine, meat, fish, and sexual union.

The Dakshina Marga (right-handed path) follows more conformist practices, focusing on mantra, yantra, and well-defined processes for spiritual growth. There is no wrong path in Tantra, but, in modern times, the Kaula Marga has been at the receiving end of a great deal of flak as it is grossly misrepresented, especially by Western theologians who do not quite understand the subtleties of ancient Hindu Vedic texts.

Mishra Tantra is a school where both external and internal practices are combined; worship is done using rituals and mental practices. While the rituals continue to include mandala, yantra, and herbs, here they are combined with asana, pranayama, dharana, and dhyana. The focus here is mainly on awakening the Anahata or the heart chakra, and the eventual desire is to remove dependence on all external objects of worship and wholly channel it inward.

Samaya is considered the loftiest school of Tantra, as we now move from the gross aspects of worship to the most subtle. Here, the practices are purely internal, with no external objects or rituals. Yogic practices such as asana, pranayama, dhyana, and Samadhi are emphasized, and the human body is seen as a yantra and worshipped accordingly. The Sahasrara chakra is the main object of focus in this school of Tantra.

As humans, we continually evolve, learn, and change with every life experience. Every life experience can either be an external one or an internal one. Based on how the energies move in any specific experience, there is a corresponding change in the state of awareness. An experience that occurs due to the sense organs is an example of outward-moving energy. For example, our desire to enjoy food or drink leads us to seek fulfilment of this desire through external sources. Therefore, we can see this energy movement as outward and downward since it further entangles us in the snare of Maya, or illusion.

On the other hand, when we seek fulfilment from within by involving ourselves in practices such as chanting, meditation, mindfulness, or prayer, we can see that the energy movement is inward and upward. We are now slowly disentangling ourselves from the veil of ignorance as we move towards spiritual growth and development.

Based on this movement of energy (outward and downward or inward and upward), Tantra texts define two paths that any individual may take in his life journey:

Pravritti Marga (The Natural Path)

This is the path of the outward movement of energy that leads us to the world of activity, seeking enjoyment and fulfilment, and having an extroverted nature with normal and natural social interactions. People on this path live as householders, fulfilling their obligations and responsibilities with perhaps an inkling of the understanding that all they seek is transient and impermanent.

Nivritti Marga (The Source Path)

This is the path of the inward movement of energy that a person who wishes to become one with the source embraces. It is the path of the renunciate or the hermit, and yet, it does not mean one has to withdraw from society or community. It only requires developing a gradual disinterest in all material and worldly pleasures.

In Tantra, Shakti is secret and subtle. She only reveals herself to the seeker after years of intense devotion and sadhana. Shakti, therefore, compromises the inner guiding light, knowledge, and comprehension. Hence, Shakti is Vidya. "In Tantra, the world is not something to escape from or overcome, but rather, even the mundane or seemingly negative events in day-to-day life are beautiful and auspicious," says Pure Yoga founder Rod Stryker, a teacher in the Tantra tradition. "Rather than looking for Samadhi, or liberation from the world, Tantra teaches that liberation is possible in the world by emphasizing personal experimentation and experience as a way to move forward on the path to self-realization."

Shri Aghorinath Ji writes: Tantra can also be understood to mean 'to weave, to expand, and to spread', and according to tantric masters, the fabric of life can provide true and everlasting fulfilment only when all the threads are woven according to the pattern designated by nature. When we are born, life naturally forms itself around that pattern. But as we grow, our ignorance, desire, attachment, fear, and false images of others and ourselves tangle and tear the threads, disfiguring the fabric. Tantra sadhana, or practice, reweaves the fabric and restores the original pattern. This path is systematic and comprehensive. The profound science and practices pertaining to hatha yoga, pranayama, mudras, rituals, kundalini yoga, nada yoga, mantra, mandala, visualization of deities, alchemy, Ayurveda, astrology, and hundreds of esoteric practices for generating worldly and spiritual prosperity blend perfectly in the tantric disciplines."

Dasa Mahavidya and Tantra are intimately linked within the Shakta tradition. The Mahavidya are considered the focal deities of tantric worship. The Mahavidya, as aspects or emanations of Shakti, represent different aspects of cosmic energy, ranging from the fierce and destructive to the nurturing and benevolent. Tantric practitioners seek to awaken and harmonize these aspects within themselves, ultimately realizing their divine nature. In tantra, the Mahavidya are worshipped individually or as a collective through rituals and practices specific to each goddess. These practices involve the recitation of mantras, visualization, and meditation on the form and qualities of the chosen Mahavidya.

Tantra recognizes the interplay and integration of opposing forces, or polarities. The Mahavidya embody various aspects of existence, including creation and destruction, light and darkness, compassion and fierceness, and knowledge and ignorance. By worshipping and meditating upon the Mahavidya, tantric practitioners seek to integrate and harmonize these polarities within themselves, leading to spiritual growth and self-realization. The Mahavidya emphasize non-dualistic philosophy, which recognizes the underlying unity of all things by encompassing seemingly opposing qualities within themselves. They remind us of the underlying unity and interconnectedness of existence.

The Mahavidya serve as powerful archetypes that guide tantric aspirants in their spiritual journey. Through their worship, practitioners aim to transcend dualities, dissolve limitations, and access higher states of consciousness. The Mahavidya, with their diverse attributes, help practitioners explore and integrate the multifaceted aspects of existence, while Tantra provides a comprehensive framework for sadhana and the exploration of the transformative powers represented by the Mahavidya. Together, they offer a path of spiritual evolution, empowering practitioners to merge with the divine feminine energy and realize their inherent divinity.

Kali – The Devourer of Time

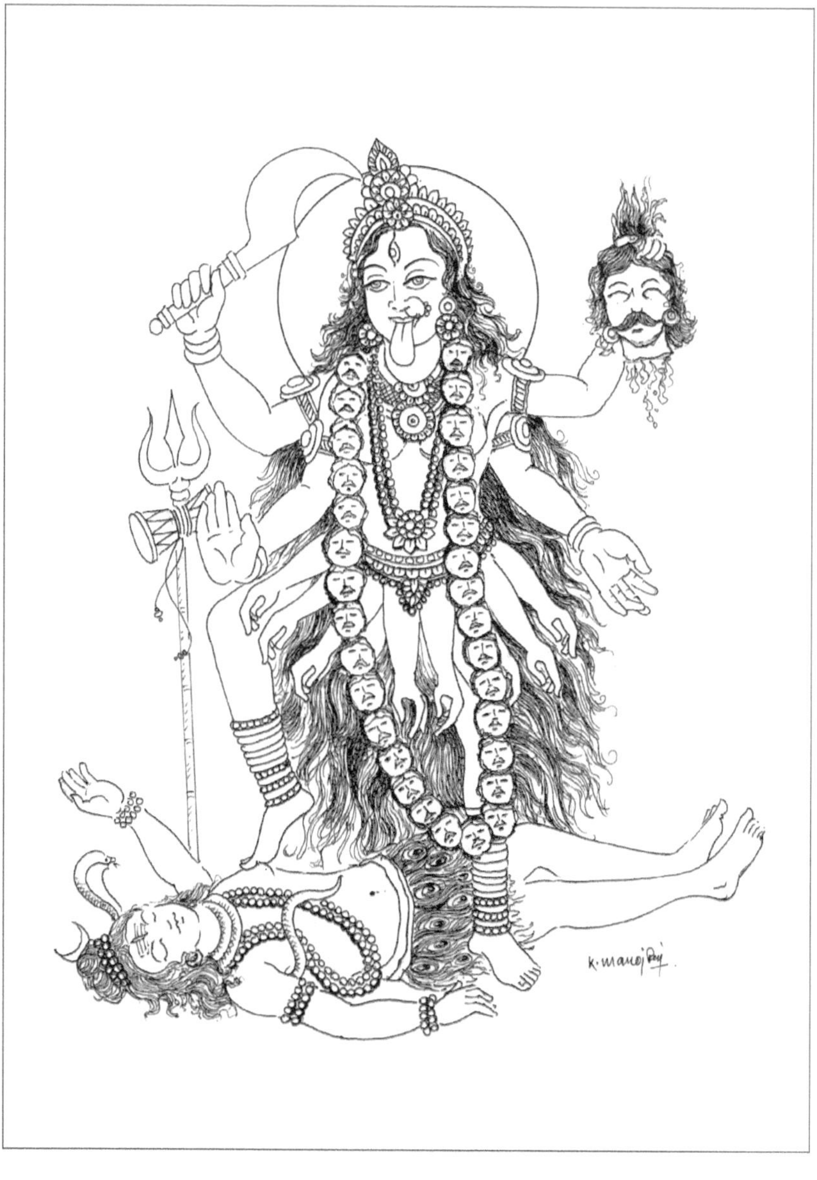

*Karala-badanam ghoram mukta keshim chaturbhuryam
Kalikam dakshinam dibyam munda-mala bibhushitam
Sadya-chinna shira kharga bama-dordha karambujam
Abhayam baradan-chaiba dakshina-dardha panikam

Fierce of face, she is dark, with flowing hair and has four-arms
Adorned with a garland of heads
In Her left hands she holds a severed head and a sword
She bestows sanctuary and blessings with her right hands.

Every chapter starts with the dhyana mantra of the goddess. Dhyana mantras are recited to sonically invoke and mentally visualize the subtle forms of deities before meditation and worship.

Kali is Adimahavidya, the first of the ten great wisdom goddesses in the Tantric tradition. Kali is listed first not to imply hierarchy but to establish the idea of order in cosmic evolution as she is the one who "spins the wheel of universal time". When there were neither the sun nor the moon, the planets nor the earth, there was only darkness, and everything was created from this darkness. At the end of the manifested world, time (Kala) devours all the universes of the three plans of creation: the physical, the astral, and the causal universes. Kali finally devours Kala thereby becoming the primordial cause of and destruction, and creation thereafter, of the universe.

In the Mahanirvana Tantra, Shiva describes Kali thus:

"At the dissolution of things, it is Kala who will devour all, and by reason of this he is called Mahakala, and since thou devourest Mahakala himself, it is thou who art the Supreme Primordial Kalika.

Because Thou devourest Kala, thou art Kali, the original form of all things, and because thou art the origin of and devourer of all things, thou art called the Adya (the Primordial One).

Re-assuming after dissolution thine own form, dark and formless, thou alone remains as the ineffable and inconceivable Kali.

Though having a form, yet art thou formless; though thyself are without beginning, multiform by the power of Maya, thou art the beginning of all, creatrix, protector, and destroyer that thou art."

The word Kala denotes time in Sanskrit. In the Vedic tradition, time is seen as both linear and cyclic. It is linear in the sense that it moves forward and is never-ending, but it is also cyclic because it is believed to repeat itself in an eternal cycle of creation and destruction. This concept of cyclic time is called Kalachakra. In this worldview, the universe goes through four ages, or yugas, which repeat in a cycle: the Satya Yuga, the Treta Yuga, the Dwapara Yuga, and the Kali Yuga. These yugas are characterized by different levels of morality, spirituality, and righteousness, with the Kali Yuga being the lowest and the Satya Yuga being the highest.

The deity Kala is believed to be the lord of time and the measurer of the lifetimes of all living beings. He is often depicted holding a noose, which symbolizes the binding of all creatures by the constraints of time. Kala is seen as a destroyer of all

Time is also closely tied to the concept of karma, which states that every action has consequences in the form of future experiences. It is believed that one's actions in the present determine their fate in the future, and that time is the mechanism by which these consequences play out. This idea of time as the mediator of karma helps to reinforce the importance of living a moral and virtuous life in the Vedic tradition.

While Kala represents the abstract concept of time, Kali personifies the dynamic and transformative nature of time. Kala and Kali are inseparable and interconnected. Kali is considered to be the embodiment of Kala's power and energy. Kala provides the context and framework for Kali's manifestations, and Kali, in turn, expresses the intense and transformative aspects of time.

"Goddess Kali symbolizes the eternal dance of life and death. She teaches us that destruction is necessary for creation and that letting go of attachments leads to true liberation and spiritual growth." Says Dr. Devdutt Pattanaik, renowned mythologist and author.

Kali's origins can be traced back to ancient Hindu texts such as the Devi Mahatmya and the Kalika Purana. Although the word kali appears as early as the Atharva Veda, the first use of it as a proper name is in the Kathaka Grhya Sutra. According to

David Kinsley, Kali is mentioned in Hindu tradition as a distinct goddess around 600 AD, and these texts usually place her on the periphery of society or on the battlefield.

Her most well-known appearance is on the battlefield in the sixth century, as Devi Mahatmaya. The deity of the first chapter of Devi Mahatmaya is Mahakali, who appears from the body of sleeping Vishnu as goddess Yoga Nidra to wake him up in order to protect Brahma and the world from two asuras, Madhu and Kaitabha. Vishnu wakes up and starts a war against them. After a long battle, Vishnu admits that he is not able to defeat the two demons. Mahakali emerges from the body of Vishnu in the form of Mahamaya to enchant the two asuras. When Madhu and Kaitabha are kept occupied by Mahakali, Vishnu succeeds in killing them.

The Devi Mahatmaya narrates the story of Kali appearing out of Durga's forehead to kill the asuras Chanda and Munda. Durga responds to an attack by these asuras with such anger that it causes her face to turn dark, resulting in Kali appearing out of her forehead. Kali's appearance is dark blue; she is gaunt with sunken eyes, wears a tiger skin sari and a garland of human heads. She defeats the two asuras.

Later in the same battle, the asura Raktabija is undefeated because of his ability to replicate himself from every drop of his blood that touches the ground. Innumerable Raktabija clones appear on the battlefield. Kali eventually defeats him by drinking his blood before it can reach the ground and consuming the numerous clones. Kinsley writes that Kali in all of these manifestations, represents "Durga's personified wrath, her embodied fury". She also appears in the Mahabharata, where she is called Kalaratri (literally, "dark blue night") and reveals herself to the Pandava soldiers in their dreams.

Iconographically, there are many varied depictions of the different forms of Kali. The most common form shows her with four arms and hands, displaying aspects of both creation and destruction. The two right hands are often held out in blessing, one in the abhaya mudra(gesture related to dispelling of fear), the other in varada mudra (gesture related to conferring boons). Her left hands hold a severed head and a blood-covered sword. The sword severs the bondage of ignorance and ego, represented by the severed head.

In other forms, she is portrayed with multiple arms, usually ten, each holding a different weapon or symbol. Her most iconic weapon is the curved sword or scimitar, known as the khadga, which represents divine knowledge and the cutting of ignorance.

She is depicted naked, as she is beyond the covering of Maya since she is pure (nirguna). She has no permanent qualities; she will continue to exist even when the universe ends. It is therefore believed that the concepts of colour, light, good, and bad do not apply to her. Her nudity symbolizes her transcendence of societal norms and the limitations of the material world.

Her free, long, black hair represents nature's freedom from civilization. Kali's tongue is often shown protruding, symbolizing her power to consume and devour negative forces. The most widespread interpretation of Kali's extended tongue involves her embarrassment over the sudden realization that she has stepped on her husband's chest. Kali's sudden shame over that act is the prevalent interpretation in Orissa. The widely recognized expression of lajja, or modesty, that Kali is expressing is depicted by the image of her biting the tongue.

Her dark complexion represents the primordial energy of the universe and the infinite potentiality that exists within it, highlighting the darkness from which everything was born. Her dark colour also represents that she is nirguna, beyond all qualities of nature.

She wears a garland of severed heads, representing the ego and the individual identities that bind humans. The garland is variously enumerated at one hundred and eight (an auspicious number in Hinduism and the number of countable beads on a japa mala) or fifty-one, representing the Varnamala or the garland of letters of the Sanskrit alphabet, Devanagari. Each of these letters represents a form of energy, and therefore she is seen as the mother of language and all mantras. She is depicted wearing a skirt made of human arms, symbolizing her power and her role as the ultimate liberator. The severed arms represent her devotee's karma that she has taken on.

Manblunder explains that the chopped hands represent the destruction of the karmas of those who have surrendered to Her. He writes: "In the short span of human existence, one's ego plays an important role. Unless one's ego is destroyed, realization is not possible. When She is prayed for in the right way, She removes one's ego. This is symbolically expressed through the chopped head. The sickle represents Her Grace, and the chopped head represents one's ego."

Kali's twin earrings are small embryos. This is because she likes devotees who have childlike qualities in them. She is shown standing with her right foot on Shiva's chest. This represents an episode where Kali goes completely out of control on the battlefield, and is about to destroy the entire universe. Shiva pacifies her by lying down under her foot to calm her. Shiva is sometimes shown with a blissful smile on his face. In this imagery, Kali is seen as dark as the night, dancing over Shiva's inert, white body. This representation reveals the significance of the two fundamental aspects of Reality: on the one hand, there is the dynamic, immanent aspect of God (Kali's dance), and on the other, the static, transcendent aspect of consciousness (identified with Shiva). Shiva is white because he signifies the infinite divine light (Prakasha), inert because the absence of movement and action reveals the consciousness as pure, homogenous, and compact. On the other hand, Kali's dance signifies the dynamic, active aspect of the Divine, and the dark color of her skin indicates that the processes of creation are dissolved in Kali.

Kali's wild and untamed appearance represents her uncontrollable power and her ability to transcend conventional boundaries. "Kali is the supreme goddess who epitomizes fearlessness, fierce love, and the ultimate truth. She is the force that annihilates darkness and brings about the light of knowledge and spiritual awakening." Dr. Nicholas Sutton, scholar of Hindu philosophy and religion.

Despite her fearsome appearance, Kali is also revered as a healer and protector. She is believed to have the power to ward off evil forces, diseases, and negative influences. Devotees seek her blessings to overcome obstacles, find inner strength, and obtain spiritual guidance. Kali is considered a compassionate mother who fiercely defends her devotees and helps them navigate life's challenges.

The spiritual significance of Kali is that each human being is both good and bad, and these energies constantly fight for supremacy. Kali grants her support and help to those who ask for it and worship her, so that the spiritual forces develop and gain supremacy over the dark, negative influences of the psychic and mental. "Kali is the divine feminine force that represents the power of transformation, destruction, and liberation. She is the embodiment of fierce compassion and the destroyer of ego and ignorance." Says Dr. David Frawley, author and expert in Hinduism.

Kali's worship has given rise to numerous regional manifestations and variations. For example, in Bengal, she is revered as Dakshina Kali, a more benevolent and compassionate form. In the South, she is seen and worshipped as Chamundi. In the north-eastern state of Assam, she is worshipped as Kamakhya, the primordial energy of creation and fertility. These regional manifestations highlight the diverse interpretations and cultural significance associated with Kali.

Kali has been a Goddess who has adapted to cultural shifts and theological developments, with changing symbolism and interpretations associated with her at various times and by different traditions and practices. From her earliest depictions in ancient texts to contemporary understandings, Kali's evolution reflects the dynamism of Hindu spirituality and the multifaceted nature of divine feminine power.

In Devi Mahatmya and the Kalika Purana, she is seen as a fierce warrior, a manifestation of the Divine Mother who emerges to combat evil forces. During the medieval period, as Tantra gained prominence, Kali became a central figure, embodying both destructive and transformative energies. Tantric worship of Kali emphasized rituals, visualization, and mantra recitation to invoke her presence and harness her power for spiritual attainment.

During the Bhakti movement, which also emerged in medieval India, devotion and personal connection to deities gained significance. Kali became an object of intense devotion, with devotees emphasizing her role as the loving mother who nurtures and protects. Bhakti poets and saints composed hymns and songs extolling her divine qualities and seeking her grace.

Over time, Kali's visual representation evolved, reflecting cultural and artistic influences. In earlier depictions, she was portrayed as a fierce warrior with a terrifying appearance, while later portrayals focused more on her benevolent aspects. The symbolism of her weapons and attributes also underwent changes, adapting to regional variations and individual interpretations.

In modern times, Kali's symbolism has expanded beyond the confines of religious and cultural boundaries. Globally, various artists and spiritual seekers have embraced her. While traditional interpretations of Kali remain prevalent, new perspectives have emerged, emphasizing her feminist symbolism, her embodiment of liberation, and her relevance in addressing social and gender inequalities. Kali's popularity has transcended the Indian subcontinent, captivating the imagination of people worldwide. Her fierce and empowering imagery has resonated with individuals seeking personal transformation, strength, and spiritual liberation. She has become a symbol of resistance, challenging oppressive systems and inspiring individuals to embrace their true nature.

The evolution of Goddess Kali reflects the dynamism of Hindu mythology and the ever-evolving interpretations of divine femininity. From her ancient origins to contemporary understandings, Kali has embodied different aspects and played various roles in the spiritual and cultural landscape. Her transformative power, symbolism, and fierce persona continue to inspire and guide seekers on the path of self-realization and liberation in a changing world.

Tara – The Compassionate Star

Pratyaleeda padarpitaam-ghrishavhrid ghoratahasa para
Khadagendeevar kartri kharparbhuja hoonkarbeejodbhava
Kharvaneel vishalapingal jatajooteikanageiryuta.
Jadayam nyasya kapalike trijagatam hantyugratara swayam

Standing in the pratyalidha pose, on the heart of a corpse, supreme, ever smiling
She holds a cleaver, a blue lotus, a dagger and a bowl, chanting the mantra Hum
She is blue-hued, her hair braided with serpents, the Ugratara
She bestows all supernatural powers

Tara means star in Sanskrit, and just as a star is beautiful but perpetually self-combusting, so too is the goddess perceived as the personification of the unquenchable hunger that propels all life. The word Tara also means "the savior" if one refers to the Sanskrit root "tri", referring to "passing over", as in overcoming any obstacle such as a water body or a mountain. In other words, "Tri" contains a reference to overcoming any difficult situation. She is seen as a tantric manifestation of Parvati.

The origin story of Tara can be found in the Todala Tantra, which recounts the tale of the Churning of the Ocean (Samudra Manthan). The warrior god Indra had the responsibility of protecting the world from demons who sought to destroy it. With the assistance of the goddess Lakshmi, the deity of success and fortune, Indra successfully defended the world for many years. However, one day, a wise sage presented Indra with a garland of sacred flowers as a gift. In a moment of distraction, Indra threw the flowers away, which displeased the sage. Observing this act, and perceiving it as a display of arrogance, Lakshmi became angry and decided to punish Indra by leaving the realm of the gods and entering the depths of the Milky Ocean.

Without Lakshmi's divine power, the gods lost their blessings, and demons started infiltrating the world. Darkness enveloped everything, people grew greedier, and the gods were ignored. As time passed, the gods gradually lost their power and influence. Realizing the seriousness of the situation, Indra turned to Vishnu, the preserver of the universe, and pleaded for assistance. Vishnu instructed Indra and the other gods to churn the ocean in order to bring Lakshmi back to the surface and regain her favour. Various treasures were hidden in the depths of the ocean, including Amrita, the elixir of life, a potion which when consumed guaranteed immortality. These treasures would aid the gods in vanquishing the demons and restoring balance to the world.

For over a thousand years, the gods worked unitedly in their effort to churn the ocean, hoping to retrieve Lakshmi and the sought-after treasures. However, they encountered numerous challenges and obstacles along the way. Eventually, Lakshmi emerged from the ocean's depths as a beautiful woman standing on a lotus flower, accompanied by the long-awaited treasures. Along with the treasures, a deadly poison called Halahala also surfaced from the ocean. The poison was so potent that it threatened to destroy all creation. In order to save the universe from its devastating effects, Lord Shiva consumed the poison.

As the poison coursed through Lord Shiva's body, his complexion turned blue. To ease his pain and cool down the effects of the poison, his wife, Parvati, pressed her fingers against his throat, stopping the poison from spreading further. As a result, her fingertips turned blue, and he became known as Neelakanta (the one with a blue throat). The poison continued to affect Lord Shiva, and to alleviate his suffering, various goddesses emerged from different parts of his body. One of these goddesses was Tara, who manifested from a tear that fell from Shiva's eye.

According to the Svatantra Tantra, Tara protects her devotees from dangers (ugra) and provides relief from unforeseen miseries, so she is known as Ugra Tara. In other Tantra texts, we find references to Shyama Tara, where she is depicted as a youthful and compassionate goddess with a green complexion. Shyama Tara is believed to have the power to swiftly come to the aid of those who call upon her. The qualities associated with her are protection, healing, compassion, and liberation from fear and obstacles. Devotees often seek her blessings for overcoming challenges and attaining spiritual enlightenment. She is depicted with one leg outstretched, indicating her readiness to come to the aid of sentient beings. Shweta Tara is another revered form where she is depicted as a serene and compassionate deity with a white complexion and is associated with purity, longevity, healing, and spiritual nourishment. Shweta Tara is depicted as seated in a meditative posture with seven eyes—three on her face and one on each palm and sole of her feet. These eyes symbolize her ability to perceive the suffering of beings in all realms and respond to their needs. Devotees seek her blessings for physical and mental well-being, long life, and spiritual growth.

In appearance, Tara appears to be very similar to *Kali* and one is often confused with the other. Since Tara is the first transformation of time and of the energy of life that Kali represents, the similarity is understandable and perhaps even necessary to show the gradual evolution of Shakti from one manifestation to another. We see that both are shown as fierce goddesses with a dark complexion (Kali is depicted as black while Tara is usually seen to be blue in hue); they both are described as standing upon a supine corpse. Both are shown wearing minimal clothing; Kali wears only a girdle of severed human arms, while Tara wears a tiger skin skirt. Both wear a necklace of severed human heads. The Kalika Purana *d*escribes Tara as holding kartri (scissors), khadga (sword), a skull cup, an indivara (lotus), and a single matted braid over her head. She is dark in complexion, tall, with a bulging belly, and wears tiger pelts, with her left foot on the chest of a corpse and her right foot placed on the thighs of the corpse. She has a terrifying laugh that causes untold fear in those within hearing distance.

Tara is shown standing in the Pratyalidha stance (in which the left foot is placed forward). She is depicted as deep blue in colour, which is symbolic of the Ajna Chakra, or third eye energy, represented by this colour. She is shown with a protruding belly to depict fertility and connectedness to the physical plane.

Her consort Shiva, in the form of Akshobhya, is seen as a serpent coiled around her matted hair. One hand holds a pair of scissors, showing how she slowly cuts her devotees from the bonds of life. In one hand, she holds a broad sword, again a sign of liberating her followers. She holds a blue lotus, representative of thriving, love, evolution, and spiritual wisdom. In the other hand, she holds a skull cup representative of the Sahasrara or crown chakra energy, the highest form of spiritual consciousness

Tara is the primordial sound (sabdabrahman) from which speech originates, within the framework of Tantra. In Hinduism, the concept of sound and speech holds great significance. It is believed that the entire universe originated from sound, and this primal sound is often referred to as Sabdabrahman, the primordial sound or the divine vibration. She symbolizes the sacred syllable Om, which is considered the foundational vibration from which all creation emanates. The Mandukya Upanishad describes Om as the sound symbolizing the ultimate reality, Brahman.

The syllable Om consists of five components:

1. A (aah) - Vaishvanara: The first component of Om is represented by the sound "A" (pronounced as "aah"). It symbolizes the waking state of consciousness, known as Vaishvanara. It corresponds to the gross or physical aspect of existence, encompassing the external world and the experiences of the senses. This aspect represents the individual self (jivatman) and the material realm.

2. U (oo) - Taijasa: The second component of Om is represented by the sound "U" (pronounced "oo"). It symbolizes the dream state of consciousness known as Taijasa. It corresponds to the subtle or astral realm, where thoughts, emotions, and impressions reside. This aspect represents subtle energy, the inner world, and the dreaming mind.

3. M (mm) - Prajna: The third component of Om is represented by the sound "M" (pronounced as "mm"). It symbolizes the deep sleep state of consciousness, known as

Prajna. It corresponds to the state of rest and rejuvenation, where there are no dreams or perceptions. This aspect represents the dormant state of consciousness and the latent potential within.

4. Bindu (dot) - Turiya: The Bindu, a dot or point placed above Om, represents the fourth state of consciousness known as Turiya. It transcends the three ordinary states (waking, dreaming, and deep sleep) and represents the state of pure awareness, or the supreme consciousness (Brahman), beyond duality. It signifies the unmanifested and the ultimate reality.

5. Silence - Turiyatita: Beyond the three sounds (A, U, and M) and the Bindu, there is the aspect of silence, which represents Turiyatita—the state beyond Turiya. It is the ineffable and formless reality that exists beyond all states and descriptions. It signifies the transcendent and infinite nature of the divine.

When recited together, the syllables A, U, and M and the silence that follows represent the totality of existence, from the gross to the subtle to the transcendent.

Tara's association with Om signifies her role as the primal resonance underlying creation. Just as Om encompasses the entirety of sound, Tara symbolizes the essence of all vibrations and frequencies. She represents the harmonious resonance that sustains the universe and acts as the bridge between the manifest and unmanifest realms. Om is considered the creative force that brings forth existence. Similarly, Tara embodies the creative power of sound. She is the dynamic aspect of Shakti that initiates manifestation and transformation. Tara's association with Om signifies her role in the cosmic dance of creation, preservation, and dissolution.

Tara, in her form as the primordial sound, represents the essence of all speech and the creative power behind it. She is considered the embodiment of the divine vibration that gives rise to language, communication, and expression. It is through the power of her sound that all forms of speech, from simple conversation to the sacred hymns and mantras of Hindu rituals, manifest.

Tara, as Sabdabrahman is sometimes depicted as a goddess with a musical instrument, such as a vina or a drum, symbolizing her connection with sound and rhythm. She is associated with the cosmic vibrations that permeate the universe and the energy that underlies all verbal and non-verbal communication.

In this aspect, Goddess Tara represents the transformative power of language and sound. Through her grace, one can tap into the inherent potential of speech and communication for spiritual growth, self-expression, and attaining higher states of consciousness. By invoking her, one seeks to align with the divine vibration and access the power of the primordial sound within oneself. A devotee who attains success in her mantra is said to gain a complete understanding of all the Shastras and attain moksha. The tantric tradition asserts that devotees of Tara will have extraordinary literary talents, being able to express ideas beyond the capacities of fellow humans. In an article on Tara, the Sivashakti website states: "Tara contains within herself all existing mantras. For instance, in order to be able to use and assimilate correctly the spiritual meaning of a mantra that synthesizes a very elevated macrocosmic aspect and in order to be able to identify ourselves with the subtle energy of a mantra, the grace of The Great Cosmic Force Tara is indispensable."

It is said that attaining Tara's grace (anugraha) is much easier than attaining the grace of the other Goddesses of Dasa Mahavidya, as there are no restrictions (niyama) on worshiping her. Tara is said to be more approachable to the devotee because of her maternal instincts, since Shiva himself assumes the position of an infant vis-à-vis the goddess. Therefore, the

Goddess, who is Mother to Shiva himself, provides Moksha to human beings irrespective of their Karma. Dr. Thomas Coburn, professor of religious studies and author specializing in Hinduism, writes: "Goddess Tara is the embodiment of compassion and the divine mother. She represents the nurturing and protective aspects of the feminine energy, offering solace, guidance, and liberation to her devotees."

Tara is seen as the Shakti who ferries Her devotees across the worldly ocean.

Tarayati Anaya Sa – Tara

Tara frees her devotees from the three miseries, also known as the threefold sufferings or tri-dukha concept, which refers to the fundamental experiences of suffering or dissatisfaction that are inherent to human existence. These three miseries are:

1. Daihika Dukha (Physical Suffering): Daihika dukkha refers to the suffering associated with the physical body. It encompasses various forms of physical pain, discomfort, illness, and the inevitable decay and mortality of the body. This suffering arises from factors such as disease, old age, injuries, and bodily limitations. The physical body, being subject to impermanence and vulnerability, is prone to suffering in the form of physical ailments and limitations.

2. Daivika Dukha (Divine Suffering): Daivika dukha refers to the suffering caused by external or divine factors. It encompasses the experiences of suffering that are believed to arise from fate, destiny, or the influence of celestial forces. This suffering is often seen as beyond human control and is attributed to karmic influences, past actions, or the interplay of cosmic forces. Examples of daivika dukha can include natural disasters, calamities, personal

misfortunes, and the experience of unfavourable life circumstances.

3. Bhautika Dukha (Suffering from Living Beings): Bhautika dukha refers to the suffering arising from interactions with other living beings. This includes the suffering resulting from disputes, relationships, social dynamics, and the inherent difficulties in human interactions. Bhautika dukha encompasses suffering such as emotional distress, relational conflicts, societal inequalities, and the challenges of navigating human relationships. It recognizes that interactions with other living beings can be a source of suffering due to misunderstandings, attachments, expectations, and the complex nature of human existence.

These three miseries reflect the understanding that suffering is an intrinsic part of human life. They highlight the various dimensions of suffering that individuals may encounter, including physical, metaphysical, and interpersonal aspects. The goal in Hindu philosophy and spiritual practices is to transcend these sufferings through self-realization, detachment, and the pursuit of spiritual liberation.

The goddess Tara can therefore be invoked in situations of difficulty or when we need to make a decision and are not sure about the outcomes. Tara is the Polar Star, providing us inspiration and acting as our guide on the path of spiritual freedom. Dr. Shantilal Nagar, scholar of Hinduism and Tantra, says: "Goddess Tara is the embodiment of fearlessness and swift, compassionate action. She is the motherly figure who shields her devotees from all forms of fear and distress, enabling them to embark on their spiritual journeys with courage and determination."

Tara represents the compassionate aspect of enlightened wisdom. Her teachings emphasize the cultivation of compassion, kindness, and empathy towards all beings. She is known for her swift response to the needs of her devotees. Tara is a powerful embodiment of feminine energy, inspiring and empowering women, symbolizing their strength, resilience, and spiritual potential. Tara encourages women to embrace their innate wisdom and compassion, fostering their spiritual growth and self-realization by overcoming the inner obstacles of ignorance, delusion, and negative emotions. She helps practitioners navigate the challenges of life, guiding them towards clarity, wisdom, and inner peace.

Tara is associated with the sacred River Ganga. She is believed to reside in the Ganga's waters and is considered its divine guardian. Devotees seek her blessings and purification by taking holy dips in the Ganga, invoking her presence and grace. She is the Mahavidya associated with planet Jupiter, and therefore discipline is required to acquire her grace, as Jupiter is a strict teacher and demands rituals, purity, sanctity, and respect. While Tara is primarily associated with Hinduism, she is also a significant figure in Tibetan Buddhism. In Tibetan Buddhist traditions, Tara is revered as a Bodhisattva, an enlightened being who embodies compassion and wisdom. She is considered one of the most important female deities in Tibetan Buddhism and is revered for her swift and compassionate assistance to those in need.

Lalita Tripura Sundari – The Divine Beauty

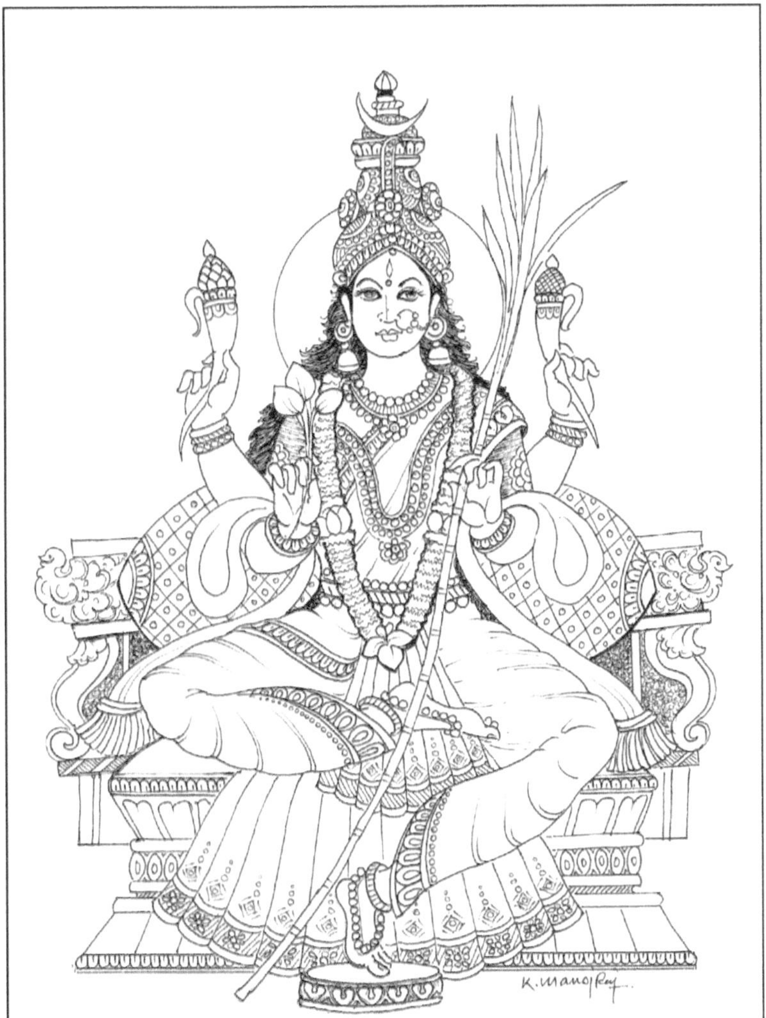

Sinduraruna vigraham trinayanam manikya mauli sphurat
Tara nayaka shekharam smita mukhi mapina vakshoruham
Panibhyam alipoorna ratna chashakam raktotpalam bibhratim
Saumyam ratna ghatastha rakta charanam dhyayet param
ambikam

Dhyayet padmasana stitham vikasitavadanam padmapatraya
takshim
Hemabham pitavastram karakalitalasad hema padmam varangim
Sarvalankara yuktam satata mabhayadam bhaktanamram
bhavanim
Srividyam shanta murtim sakala suranutam sarva sampat
pradatrim

The Divine Mother is to be meditated upon as shining in a vermilion-red body with three eyes, sporting a crown of rubies studded with the crescent moon, a face all smiles, a splendid bust, one hand holding a jewel-cup brimming with mead and the other twirling a red lotus.

The Divine Goddess is to be meditated upon as seated on the lotus with petal eyes. She is golden-hued and has lotus flowers in her hand. She dispels the fear of the devotees who bow before Her. She is the embodiment of peace and knowledge, is praised by gods, and grants every kind of wealth sought by a devotee.

The Advaita tradition believes that the human mind needs a concrete form to understand the divine, which is impossible to define. Colour can only be understood when seen in a concrete form, not from an abstract description. In the same way, divinity can be best comprehended when described with a name and a form. And out of all the name-forms of Gods and Goddesses in Hinduism, there is none more beautiful than Lalita Tripura Sundari. Her beauty represents the divine aesthetic, the allure of spiritual enlightenment, and establishes her as an embodiment of compassion, grace, and auspiciousness.

The word Lalita refers to "the one who plays". In Hinduism, "Lila" is a concept that can be translated as divine play, sport, or game. Lila represents the belief that the universe, including all its beings and activities, is an expression of the divine in a playful and spontaneous manner. The purpose of this cosmic play is not for any specific goal or accomplishment, but rather for the pure enjoyment of the divine. The universe is seen as a playground, and all beings, including humans, animals, plants, and even deities, are seen as participants in this divine play.

In the Tantra tradition, we find references to several triads, such as the Trishakti (the three fundamental energies: Iccha shakti, Jnana shakti and Kriya shakti), the Trigunas (Tamas, Rajas, and Sattva), the Tridoshas (Vata, Pitta, and Kapha) and the Three Shariras (Sthula, Sukshma, and Karana).

Tripura (the three cities) refers to all of the above and can finally be explained as the three fundamental states of being: the state of being awake, the state of sleep with dreams, and the state of deep sleep. Lalita Tripura Sundari is the sovereign goddess of these three states of consciousness.

Sundari refers to her exquisite and supreme beauty, which can be recognized as the beauty inherent in the natural world. The descriptions of landscapes, mountains, rivers, and flora in ancient texts often emphasize their aesthetic appeal. The Rigveda expresses admiration for the beauty of nature and its connection to the divine. Beauty extends beyond the physical realm and can refer to the concept of inner beauty, characterized by virtues such as compassion, humility, and selflessness. The Bhagavad Gita extols the importance of inner beauty as Krishna describes the qualities of a spiritually awakened individual. Finally, her beauty can be considered a pathway to transcendence and spiritual realization. The concept of "Rasa" encapsulates this idea, referring to the aesthetic experience that evokes deep emotions and transports the individual beyond the material realm.

The origin story of Lalita Tripura Sundari is described in the Lalita Sahasranama and Lalitopakhyana. The Lalitopakhyana narrates the tale of a fierce battle that took place between the gods and the demons, with the latter gaining the upper hand. The gods sought the help of the divine trinity—Brahma, Vishnu, and Shiva, to defeat the powerful demon named Bhandasura. In response to their plea, Lalita Tripura Sundari appeared as an embodiment of beauty and power to destroy the Asuras.

Another legend says that Shiva constantly teased Parvati by calling her "Kali", referring to her dark complexion. She took the form of the most supreme beauty, Lalita Tripura Sundari, to show her husband that she is capable of manifesting in any form and that inner beauty is to be treasured more than mere external features. She epitomizes the beauty of pure perception that appears when we envision the whole of nature as a direct reflection of Brahman.

Lalita Tripura Sundari is depicted as a young, captivating goddess with a beautiful face, adorned with various ornaments. The Tantrasara dhyana mantra describes how she is illuminated by the jewels of the crowns of Brahma and Vishnu, which fell at her feet when they bowed down to worship her. In the Lalita

Sahasranama, a sacred text containing a thousand names of the goddess, she is described thus:

Arunam Karuna thrangitakshim dhrutha
Pasangusa pushpabana chapam
Animadhibhi ravrutham mayurai
Raha mityeva vibhavaye Bhavanim

It describes her as glowing like a rising sun as sits on a lotus, which rests on Shiva's body. She wears red silk attire and has long, flowing tresses, and her smile overwhelms Kameshwara, the lord of desire. She has a crescent moon on her forehead. In the Jnana Khanda of Tripura Rahasya, she sits on a throne which has legs featuring the Pancha Brahmas – Brahma, Vishnu, Mahesha, and Ishwara, and the platform itself representing Sadashiva. These five forms symbolize the concept of Panchamahabhuta, the five fundamental elements that constitute the physical universe. These elements are believed to be the building blocks of creation and play a crucial role in understanding the nature of reality. The Panchamahabhuta consist of the following elements:

1. Prithvi (Earth): Prithvi represents the element of solidity and is associated with the physical aspect of existence. It relates to stability, grounding, and the material realm. It symbolizes the physical body, fertility, and the realm of the senses.

2. Apa or Jala (Water): Apa or Jala signifies the element of fluidity and represents the quality of liquidity and cohesion. Water is considered essential for life, purification, and sustenance. It is associated with emotions, healing, and the realm of the heart.

3. Agni (Fire): Agni represents the element of fire and embodies the qualities of heat, transformation, and illumination. Fire is seen as a symbol of energy, passion,

and purification. It is associated with vitality, creativity, and the realm of action.

4. Vayu (Air): Vayu signifies the element of air and represents the quality of movement and expansion. Air is associated with breath, life force, and communication. It symbolizes the power of the mind, the intellect, and the realm of thought.

5. Akasha (Ether or Space): Akasha represents the element of space or ether and symbolizes the unbounded and all-pervading nature of existence. It is associated with openness, expansion, and consciousness. Akasha is considered the space in which all other elements exist and interact.

These five elements are not only seen as external forces but are also believed to exist within the human body, influencing both the physical and subtle aspects of our being. The Panchamahabhuta concept finds its application in various aspects of Hindu philosophy, including Ayurveda (the traditional Indian system of medicine), Vastu Shastra (the science of architecture), and Yoga. Understanding and harmonizing these elements is seen as a means to achieve balance, health, and spiritual evolution.

In the context of the throne of Lalita Tripura Sundari, Brahma signifies the earth element and the activity of creation. Vishnu is the water element and the activity of preservation. Mahesha is the fire element and the activity of destruction and transformation, while Ishwara represents the air element and the activity of concealment (Shiva's action of hiding his essential nature). Sadashiva stands for the most subtle of all the elements, ether (Akasha Mahabhuta), and symbolizes Shiva's grace.

Lalita Tripura Sundari is depicted with four arms, representing her ability to manifest and control the four aspects of existence: creation, preservation, destruction, and grace. She holds a bow with five flowery arrows in one hand. Metaphorically,

Tripura Sundari hunts her devotees down with the arrows of delight by revealing, through the five senses, the various forms of creation as aspects of our inner divine nature.

In another hand, she holds a sugarcane bow, which personifies the mind that is characterised by Sankalpa and Vikalpa. While Sankalpa refers to how one thinks, Vikalpa points to the difference of perception or choice. When we allow Lalita Tripura Sundari to rule over our minds, we can understand the sweetest reality of the Brahman, just as we can enjoy the sweetest juice of the sugarcane.

The noose that she carries represents how she can tug away the desires of her devotees using the rope. It is also symbolic of how she is able to bring her worshippers closer to her, helping them get rid of attachments. The goad symbolizes repulsion, pointing both to her ability to cut through ignorance and guide devotees towards spiritual enlightenment.

She is often depicted in popular iconography as a sixteen year old girl (hence "Shodashi") and in this manifestation she embodies the concept of "Shodasha Kama," which refers to the sixteen types of desires that are considered fundamental to human existence. These desires encompass a wide range of human needs, urges and inclinations. They are:

1. Dharma Kama: Desire for righteousness, moral values, and ethical conduct

2. Artha Kama: Desire for material wealth, prosperity, and success

3. Moksha Kama: Desire for liberation, spiritual enlightenment, and self-realization

4. Prema Kama: Desire for love, affection, and emotional connection

5. Sampatti Kama: Desire for good fortune, auspiciousness, and favourable circumstances

6. Puja Kama: Desire for worship, devotion, and engaging in religious rituals

7. Yasha Kama: Desire for fame, reputation, and recognition

8. Vriddhi Kama: Desire for growth, progress, and expansion in various aspects of life

9. Jaya Kama: Desire for victory, triumph, and accomplishment

10. Danda Kama: Desire for justice, fairness, and righteous punishment

11. Niti Kama: Desire for ethical conduct, moral principles, and virtuous behaviour

12. Kula Kama: Desire for maintaining family, lineage, and ancestral traditions

13. Rupa Kama: Desire for beauty, aesthetics, and attractiveness

14. Vaya Kama: Desire for youthfulness, vitality, and physical well-being

15. Bala Kama: Desire for strength, power, and energy

16. Pravritti Kama: Desire for worldly engagements, social interactions, and participation in societal activities

These sixteen desires represent different aspects of human nature and aspirations, acknowledging the multidimensionality of human existence. They are not inherently negative or detrimental; rather, they are seen as natural inclinations that can be harnessed and directed in a balanced and harmonious way.

The form of Shodashi emphasizes the importance of understanding and fulfilling these desires in a righteous and ethical manner, without getting attached to, or driven solely by them. The ultimate aim is to cultivate a state of inner harmony, spiritual growth, and realization of one's true nature, transcending the limitations of worldly desires.

Lalita Tripura Sundari represents the moon as the visible embodiment of transcendent beauty and happiness. Shodashi is therefore associated with the sixteen phases of the moon, which are deeply rooted in the symbolism and mystical significance attributed to the lunar cycle in Hinduism. The waxing and waning of the moon throughout the month reflect the cyclical nature of existence and the ever-changing aspects of life.

In the Sri Vidya tradition, the sixteen phases of the moon are equated with the sixteen syllables of the Sri Vidya mantra, known as the Shodashakshari mantra. The lunar phases represent different energies and attributes associated with Shodashi. For example, the waxing crescent moon represents the goddess as a young maiden, while the full moon represents her in her radiant and complete form. Similarly, the waning crescent moon represents her as the aging aspect, and the new moon represents the transcendental and formless nature of the goddess.

Each syllable represents a specific aspect of the goddess. These sixteen aspects, combined with the corresponding lunar phases, symbolize the complete spectrum of the goddess's divine manifestations and qualities. The worship and meditation on Shodashi in the Sri Vidya tradition involve the understanding and embodiment of these sixteen aspects of the goddess. Devotees aim to connect with and invoke the specific energies associated with each lunar phase and corresponding aspect of Shodashi.

The connection between Shodashi and the sixteen phases of the moon signifies the integration of lunar symbolism and the divine feminine. It represents the understanding that the goddess's manifestations are as diverse and ever-changing as the phases of the moon, and that her grace and blessings are accessible throughout the entire lunar cycle.

Lalita Tripura Sundari is closely associated with the Sri Chakra, a sacred geometric diagram representing divine cosmic energy. The Sri Chakra is composed of nine interlocking triangles, four pointing upward (representing the masculine aspect) and five pointing downward (representing the feminine aspect). These triangles intersect to form forty three smaller triangles, representing the various aspects of creation and the divine energies.

At the centre of the Sri Chakra is the Bindu, a dot representing the supreme reality, or Brahman. Surrounding the Bindu are concentric circles known as the mandalas, which symbolize different levels of existence, from the microcosmic to the macrocosmic.

The Sri Chakra is considered a potent tool for meditation and spiritual practice. It is believed to represent the divine presence, and worshiping or meditating upon it is thought to lead to profound spiritual experiences and inner transformation. The intricate geometry of the Sri Chakra is seen as a blueprint of the cosmos and a visual representation of the interplay of divine energies.

Lalita Tripura Sundari is specifically associated with the central Bindu within the Sri Chakra. She is considered the residing deity of the Sri Chakra, and her form is believed to manifest within it. Lalita Tripura Sundari can be worshipped through the Sri Chakra which acts as a means to connect with the embodiment of primordial energy. Devotees engage in the meditation of the Sri Chakra, using it as a focal point for concentration and visualization. By contemplating the geometric patterns and reciting the associated mantras, practitioners seek to awaken and align themselves with the energies represented by the yantra.

Sri Vidya is a sacred tradition, or sampradaya, within Hinduism that specifically focuses on the worship of Lalita Tripura Sundari. It is considered a highly esoteric and profound path of spiritual practice centred around the revered and secretive tradition passed down through lineages of qualified gurus who transmit the knowledge and practices to sincere seekers.

Sri Vidya involves worshiping Tripura Sundari through different rituals and ceremonies, such as reciting sacred mantras like the Lalita Sahasranama, Trishati, Khadgamala, Saundarya Lahiri, and Sri Suktam; performing elaborate yantra rituals like Abhishekam and Tarpanam to the Maha Meru; and doing devotional practices like Homams (fire ritual).

The central focus of Sri Vidya is the Sri Chakra worshipped in the form of a two dimensional yantra or as a Mahameru in its three dimensional form. The teachings of Sri Vidya encompass not only the external practices and rituals but also the inner contemplation and meditation on the divine qualities and attributes of Tripurasundari. It involves understanding the symbolism and significance of the goddess's various forms and aspects and internalizing those qualities within oneself.

The most important text of Tripura Sundari is the Lalita Sahasranama, a part of the Brahmanda Purana, one of the eighteen major Puranas in Hindu scriptures. It is a conversation between the sage Agastya and king Hayagriva, an incarnation of Lord Vishnu. In this dialogue, Agastya seeks spiritual knowledge from Hayagriva, who reveals the thousand names of Lalita Tripura Sundari and their significance. Each name in the Lalita Sahasranama reflects a specific aspect, quality, or attribute, describing her divine nature, powers, and cosmic manifestations. The names are rich in poetic beauty and carry deep symbolic meaning. They highlight the various dimensions of the goddess, including her beauty, grace, compassion, wisdom, and her role as the supreme ruler of the universe.

The Lalita Sahasranama is considered a sacred and powerful chant that invokes the presence and blessings and serves as a source of inspiration, guidance, and contemplation. It is believed that by repeating these names with devotion and understanding, one can experience a deep connection with the goddess and attain spiritual upliftment. The Lalita Sahasranama is not just a devotional hymn but also a philosophical text, providing insights into the nature of divinity and the paths to spiritual realization.

Dr. David Frawley, a renowned Hindu scholar and author, says: "Lalita Tripura Sundari represents the highest form of divine feminine energy, embodying grace, beauty, and supreme wisdom. Her worship leads to the revelation of the Divine Self and brings profound joy and fulfilment in every aspect of life."

In order for us to perceive true beauty, it is important to let go of preconceived ideas and memories. Worshiping Tripura Sundari is a direct and secure path to realizing the Self. When our minds are filled with this divine knowledge, we find satisfaction in all that we do. Our perception is transformed, and even the simplest actions bring joy and happiness. In this state, we transcend time and space, perceiving the eternal and compassionate presence of the divine in everything around us.

Tripura Sundari combines the energies of activity (characteristic of Kali) and knowledge (characteristic of Tara), and infuses it with the bliss of supreme realization. The most direct method to attain this goal is introspection on our true identity through practices like self-inquiry ("Who am I?") until we realize that things around us are not separate, as they share the same source and essential nature.

The concept of Lalita emphasizes the idea of non-attachment and the transient nature of the world. It suggests that just as a player engages in a game without being overly attached to the outcome, individuals should approach life with a similar attitude. It encourages individuals to participate in the activities of the world while understanding that they are temporary and ever-changing.

The idea of Lalita provides a framework to understand the diversity and complexity of the world while recognizing the underlying unity of all existence. Lalita is an indication that human suffering is a mere illusion, a result of false knowledge rooted in our ignorance and ego. Lalita, as an image of beauty and bliss, invites us to appreciate and celebrate the beauty and diversity of creation while recognizing the divine essence that permeates it.

Understanding these truths attracts the overwhelming grace of Tripura Sundari, preparing our body, heart, and mind to experience eternal and infinite bliss. Lalita Tripura Sundari is the embodiment of conscious grace — joyful, peaceful, abundant, protective, wise, and powerful. Engaging in her worship and seeking the source of knowledge as an observer, acting out of divine will, combines the paths of devotion (bhakti), knowledge (jnana), and action (karma).

Bhuvaneshwari – The Queen of the Universe

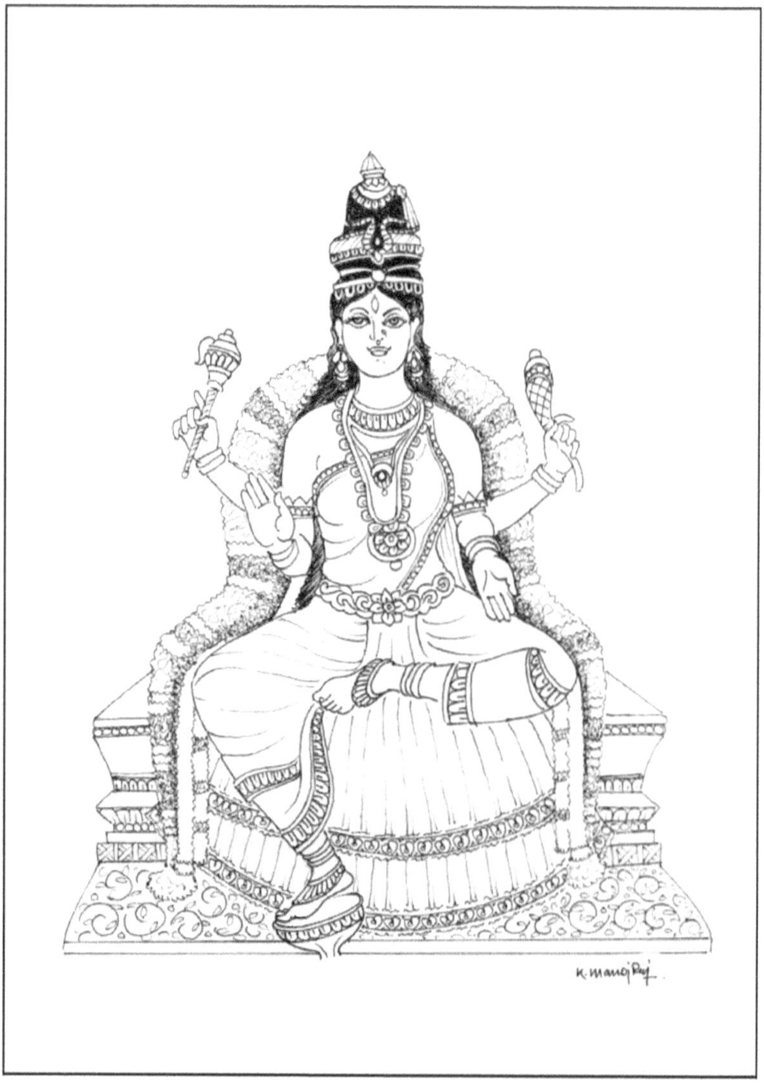

Udyad dina dyutim indu kiritaam
Tunga kucham nayana trayayuktaam
Smera mukhim varada angkusha paashaam
Abhiti karaam prabhaje bhuvaneshim

Salutations to Devi Bhuvaneshwari

Who has the splendour of the rising sun of the day

Who holds the moon on her crown like an ornament
Who has high breasts and three eyes
who has a smiling face and shows the varada mudra

Holds a hook and a noose
and displays the abhaya mudra

Salutations to Devi Bhuvaneshwari

In the Rigveda, Aditi is described as the cosmic mother of the gods (Adityas), depicted as a goddess of infinite space, representing boundlessness and fertility, and associated with protection, forgiveness, and motherly care. In the Shakta tradition, Bhuvaneshwari specifically embodies this aspect of the cosmic mother and the ruler of the entire cosmos, as she is seen as the source of the origin of all manifestation - primordial space.

The Tantric texts describe that before anything came into existence, it was the sun that appeared in the heavens. With the blessings of Lalita Tripura Sundari, the three worlds came into existence. Bhuvaneshwari, associated with the energy underlying creation, remains un-manifest until the world is created and then assumes a form appropriate to suit the manifested worlds. In this form, she came to be known as the ruler of all the Universe and as a result, is related to the visible and material aspects of the created world, seen both as a part of creation and pervading its aftermath.

Bhuvaneshwari is a Sanskrit word composed of two terms: Bhuvana and Ishwari. Bhuvan denotes the different worlds that make up the universe, and Ishwari is the feminine term for lord or ruler. Bhuvaneshwari is the ruler of the Tri-Bhuvana, or three regions of the Universe. The Tri-Bhuvana concept finds its roots in the Rigveda and the Upanishads, which delve into cosmology and metaphysics and refers to the three realms that constitute the universe. These realms are Bhuh (Earth), Bhuvah (Space), and Svah (Heavens).

Bhuh (Earth): Bhuh represents the physical realm, or the terrestrial world. It encompasses the earthly plane, including the land, oceans, mountains, forests, and all forms of life that exist on Earth. It is the realm where human beings and other living creatures reside and experience worldly existence.

Bhuvah (Space): Bhuvah refers to the celestial or atmospheric region above the Earth. It is associated with the intermediate space or the realm between the Earth and the heavens. Bhuvah is considered to be the abode of celestial beings, divine energies, and subtle forces. It is associated with the realm of the mind, emotions, and spiritual energies.

Svah (Heavens): Svah represents the heavenly or celestial realms beyond the Earth and the atmosphere. It is the abode of deities, gods, and higher spiritual beings. Svah is associated with divine light, purity, bliss, and transcendence. It is considered the realm of higher consciousness, where liberated souls and divine energies reside.

The Tri-Bhuvana concept signifies the interconnectedness and interdependence of these three realms, with each playing a distinct role in the cosmic order. It is not just a physical division but also represents different states of consciousness and levels of existence. It is believed that spiritual practices and ascension through various realms can lead to liberation from the cycle of birth and death.

Bhuvaneshwari is depicted as a beautiful goddess with a golden complexion. She is described as having four arms, representing her power and ability to manifest in multiple ways. In her hands, Bhuvaneshwari holds a noose and a goad representing her ability to bind negative forces and guide her devotees on the right path. In the other two hands, we see the Abhaya and Varada mudras. The Abhaya Mudra is a gesture of fearlessness and protection, formed by raising the right hand with the palm facing outward, fingers extended upwards, and the thumb touching the base of the little finger. This mudra signifies the assurance of safety and security.

The Varada Mudra is the gesture of granting boons and blessings, formed by extending the open right hand downwards with the palm facing outwards. It signifies her willingness to fulfil the wishes and grant spiritual and material benefits to those who seek her intervention. She is shown seated on a lotus, which symbolizes purity, spiritual awakening, and the unfolding of consciousness. Bhuvaneshwari is adorned with majestic and regal attire, including a crown, representing her supreme status as the ruler of the universe. She wears various ornaments, such as earrings, necklaces, and bracelets, highlighting her divine beauty and grace.

Like many Hindu deities, Bhuvaneshwari is depicted with a third eye on her forehead, symbolizing her expanded consciousness, inner wisdom, and higher perception, as well as her complete knowledge of the manifested worlds. She is shown with a crescent moon adorning her forehead, representing the divine feminine energy and her connection with the cycles of nature. Her facial expression is serene and compassionate, reflecting her motherly nature and unconditional love for all beings.

Bhuvaneshwari represents infinite space, the element that permits all other elements to be created, sustained, and dissolved. It is for this reason that she is associated with the concept of the "cosmic womb," referred to as "Hiranyagarbha". "Hiranya" means golden, and "Garbha" means womb, symbolizing the potentiality, the source, and the unmanifested state of the universe before its manifestation. According to Hindu cosmological theories, the universe undergoes cycles of creation, sustenance, and dissolution, and the cosmic egg represents the unmanifested state of the universe before a new cycle of creation begins. Within the cosmic egg, all the elements and energies necessary for the formation of the universe exist in latent form.

Manblunder says in his note on Dasa Mahavidya: "Bhuvaneshwari represents akasha, or space tattva. According to the Taittiriya Upanishad, akasha is the first amongst creation: "From this comes space; from space, air; from air, fire; from fire, water; from water, earth; from earth, plants and herbs; from plants and herbs, food; and from food, human beings." Since

Bhuvaneshwari represents akasha, it is obvious that she is the cause of creation. She is also known as Vimarsa (consideration and reasoning), which also goes to prove that she is the creator."

Bhuvaneshwari is also associated with the earth element (Prithvi) and is believed to be responsible for the land's fertility, growth, and abundance. She is the creator of Prakriti, or nature. Prakriti is characterized by the three Gunas (qualities): Sattva (purity, harmony), Rajas (activity, passion), and Tamas (inertia, darkness). These Gunas are inherent in all aspects of creation, including living beings and the elements of nature. Prakriti is responsible for the formation and sustenance of natural elements, life forms, and the ebb and flow of seasons and cycles.

Prakriti is also associated with Maya, the cosmic illusion that veils the true nature of reality. Identification with Prakriti and its transient forms binds individuals to the cycle of birth and death. Moksha is attained by transcending the influence of Prakriti and realizing one's true nature as Purusha. Bhuvaneshwari is also Maya, which is explained in Lalita Sahasranama as: The root of Maya is ma. Ma means 'to measure'. Brahman is immeasurable, but due to the influence of Maya, Brahman appears to be measurable. In other words, Brahman is beyond time and space, but due to the influence of Maya, Brahman appears as if bound by time and space.

We all fall into Maya's illusory trap due to our identification with the material world and attachment to transient forms. A primary factor in falling into Maya's trap is ignorance, or Avidya. Ignorance refers to a lack of true knowledge or spiritual insight about the nature of reality, due to which we perceive the material world and its transient forms as the ultimate reality, failing to recognize the underlying divine essence.

Attachment to the material world and its objects is another factor that contributes to falling into Maya's trap. We develop strong desires and attachments towards sensory experiences, possessions, relationships, and achievements, thus perpetuating the illusion of separation and dissatisfaction. The identification with the ego or the false sense of individuality reinforces the illusory nature of Maya. Desires and cravings play a significant role in perpetuating Maya's illusory trap. We associate identity with the physical body and the fluctuating mind. Identification with the temporary aspects of the body-mind complex leads to a limited understanding of one's true nature beyond the physical and mental realms, reinforcing the illusion of separateness. One of the methods of transcending the illusion is to identify the sacred space that exists around us.

Bhuvaneshwari, who represents space, is seen as complementary to Kali, who represents Time. Bhuvaneshwari sets the stage on which Kali will perform her dance of life and death. Kali creates the events in time, and Bhuvaneshwari creates the objects in space. In Hindu cosmology, space is considered multidimensional and encompasses not only physical space but also temporal dimensions. The concept of Lokas, or realms within the universe, includes dimensions that exist beyond ordinary three-dimensional space, providing a framework that incorporates different temporal realities. Hindu rituals and sacred observances often incorporate specific time-based practices. The performance of rituals at specific astrologically determined times, such as sunrise, sunset, or specific planetary alignments, demonstrates the connection between time, cosmic order, and spiritual practices. Temples and pilgrimage sites in Hinduism are often believed to exist in sacred spaces that transcend conventional notions of time. They are considered places where the divine presence intersects with human existence, connecting the mortal realm with the eternal.

Bhuvaneshwari is also seen as the ruler of the cardinal directions, or the Dikpalas, which hold significant symbolism and spiritual significance in Tantra. These directions are considered divine guardians associated with various deities and elements and are honoured in rituals, temple architecture, and Vastu Shastra.

- The eastern direction is associated with Lord Indra, the king of gods and the ruler of the heavens. It symbolizes new beginnings, the rising sun, and enlightenment. It is often considered the direction of knowledge, wisdom, and the path towards spiritual awakening.

- The south-eastern direction is associated with Agni, the Vedic god of fire. It represents transformation, purification, and the element of fire. Agni is considered the intermediary between humans and the gods, carrying offerings from Earth to the celestial realms.

- The southern direction is associated with Yama, the god of death and lord of the underworld. It represents endings, transformation, and the cycle of life and death. Yama is seen as the keeper of dharma and is often invoked for protection and guidance on the path of righteousness.

- The south-western direction is associated with Nirrti, a goddess associated with destruction and chaos. It represents challenges, obstacles, and the need for balance. Nirrti is believed to protect against evil forces and restore equilibrium in the cosmic order.

- The western direction is associated with Varuna, the god of the cosmic ocean and the celestial waters. It represents introspection, emotions, and the element of water. Varuna is often invoked for forgiveness, mercy, and the dispelling of negative energies.

- The north-western direction is associated with Vayu, the god of wind and life force. It represents movement, change, and the breath of life. Vayu is invoked for vitality, inspiration, and spiritual progress.

- The northern direction is associated with Kubera, the god of wealth and prosperity. It represents abundance, success, and material well-being. Kubera is considered the guardian of treasures and is often worshipped for financial prosperity.

- The north-eastern direction is associated with Ishana, a form of Lord Shiva. It represents spirituality, higher consciousness, and divine grace. It is often considered the most auspicious direction and is associated with spiritual practices and meditation.

Bhuvaneshwari is represented by the bija mantra hreem, which is believed to activate and awaken the dormant feminine energy within an individual. It stimulates the chakras, particularly the Anahata (heart chakra), and facilitates the flow of love, compassion, and divine grace. Hreem is considered a protective mantra, purifying and transforming negative energies, offering a shield of divine energy to the practitioner.

Tantric texts describe that the whole macrocosm is contained in the small, subtle space located at the level of our hearts. This place in the heart is Bhuvaneshwari's residence. Dr. David Frawley explains that in the Upanishads, this secret place is known as hridayaguha, the cave of the heart. It is here that the dahara akasha, or the entire universe is held in seed form. Once we draw our awareness there, we become one with all. We move from the individual to the universal. The prime hridaya mantra is hreem, which is the root sound behind the first syllable of hridaya. Hreem is the main mantra for awakening Kundalini, as in the famous Tantric Panchadashi mantra, in which it occurs several times. We can use this mantra to draw our focus to the hridaya.

Bhuvaneshwari rules over our mental space, which can be described as the subjective realm of consciousness where thoughts, perceptions, emotions, and imagination occur. It is the internal landscape within our minds where we process information, form ideas, and experience various mental states. Our thoughts can range from mundane daily considerations to complex philosophical or abstract concepts. Mental space encompasses our subjective experience of the external world. It is where we process and interpret sensory information, such as visual, auditory, tactile, and olfactory stimuli. Perception helps us construct our understanding of reality within our mental space. It provides a canvas for imagination and creativity. It is where we can visualize and create mental images, invent new ideas, and explore alternative possibilities. Imagination allows us to go beyond the boundaries of the present moment and envision different scenarios.

Mental space also includes our ability to store and retrieve memories. It is where past experiences are stored and can be revisited through recollection. Memory helps shape our perception of the present and influences our thoughts and emotions. This space is intimately connected with our emotional states. It is where we experience and process emotions such as joy, sadness, anger, fear, and love. Emotions can colour our thoughts, influence decision-making, and shape our overall mental landscape.

This is the space where our inner dialogue takes place—a continuous stream of thoughts and self-talk that accompanies our daily lives. It is within this space that we engage in self-reflection, introspection, and self-awareness, gaining insights into our beliefs, values, and sense of self. involves our ability to direct our focus and attention. It is where we allocate cognitive resources to specific tasks, objects, or ideas while filtering out distractions. Concentration and mindfulness practices help cultivate a more focused mental space. Mental space is highly subjective and unique to each individual. It is shaped by personal experiences, beliefs, cultural influences, and individual perspectives. Our mental space is continually evolving and influenced by external factors and internal processes.

Bhuvaneshwari can be seen as the entire Universe manifested in the form of a deity representing the creative power that gives rise to the physical world. In the Dasa Mahavidya, she signifies the interconnectedness of all beings and the oneness of the universe. She represents the harmonious relationship between the physical and spiritual realms, emphasizing that everything is interconnected and interdependent. We can obtain her grace by meditating on the reality of infinite space as detached witnesses, observing the world around us without identifying with the happenings and situations.

Bhairavi – The Fierce Transformer

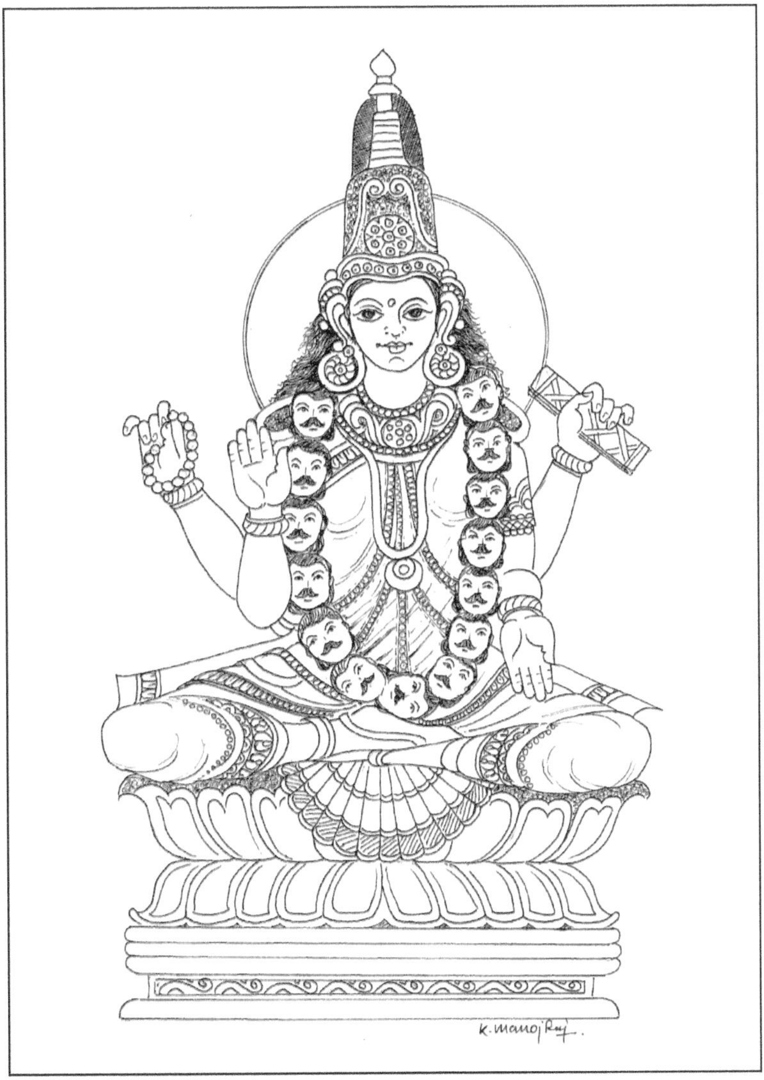

Udyadbhanu sahasra kantim arunakshaumaam shiro maalikaam

Rakta lipta payodharam japa patim vidyam abhitim varam

Hasta abjai dadhatim trinetra vilasad rakta aravinda shriyam

Devim baddha himamshu ratna mukutam vandhey samanda smitham

I meditate on Devi Bhairavi, who has the splendour of a thousand rising suns.

Who is wearing red garments and a garland of skulls
Whose breasts are smeared with blood

Who is holding a rosary and book and displaying abhiti and varada mudras

Whose three eyes are shining with the beauty of red lotuses
The Devi is wearing a red crown over her head, which is tied to the moon.

I worship Devi, Bhairavi, who is sporting a gentle smile.

The Trimurti of Brahma, Vishnu, and Shiva each embody only one function of the Universe. Brahma is responsible for creation, Vishnu for preservation, and Shiva for destruction. Bhairavi, on the other hand, represents the Brahman's extraordinary ability to create, sustain, and destroy the manifested world. While she is capable of creating and nourishing, she is most strongly related to the terrible force of destruction (of all that is evil and impure) and to the energy of the subtle universal fire, which brings about a positive transformation.

The name Bhairavi, which means that which causes terror or immense fear, comes from the Sanskrit word bhaya (fear) and embodies a captivating paradox. While its literal meaning suggests a sense of terror and dread, it transcends conventional notions of fear. Typically, fear is associated with darkness but Bhairavi's essence radiates with the brilliance of ten thousand emerging suns, captivating and awe-inspiring. She defies the darkness that instils fear in our hearts, and instead, her luminosity becomes a beacon of strength and power, inviting us to embrace the unknown with courage and wonder.

According to mythology, there was a powerful demon named Mahishasura who wreaked havoc on Earth and defeated the gods in battle. Unable to overcome him, the gods sought the help of the divine trinity—Brahma, Vishnu, and Shiva. The three deities combined their energies, and a radiant light emerged from their forms. This light transformed into a supremely powerful and fierce goddess known as Bhairavi.

Bhairavi, with her immense power and ferocity, engaged in a fierce battle with Mahishasura. When Bhairavi entered the battle field, her horrible appearance made the demons weak and fearful, and they started panicking as soon as they saw her. The battle lasted for many days, during which Bhairavi unleashed her divine weapons and fought with relentless vigour. Ultimately, she vanquished Mahishasura and restored peace and order to the universe. In some versions of the story, Bhairavi is said to have emerged from the third eye of Shiva, representing the fiery energy of transformation and destruction.

Her dhyana shloka in the Devi Mahatmaya describes her as a fierce goddess seated on a lotus. She has four hands, one with rosary beads, signifying devotion and symbolic of the unmanifest Word Para Vak; she carries a book, signifying knowledge; one hand is in abhaya mudra and another is in varada mudra. She wears red garments and a garland of severed heads around her neck. She has three eyes, and her head is adorned with a crescent moon. In another form described in the Devi Mahatmaya, she is seen carrying a sword and a cup containing blood, with her other two hands showing abhaya and varada mudras. Sometimes she is in the cremation ground, seated on a headless corpse, deeply engrossed in Shava sadhana, a particularly intense form of meditation. The main characteristic of her physical form is her radiating beauty, which is closely related to her connection with the transforming heat of Tapas and the subtle element of fire, Tejastattva.

According to the Manthana Bhairava Tantra, Tejastattva refers to the elemental power of fire, which holds significant symbolism and importance. In Tantra, Agni is one of the Pancha Bhutas (five elements) that constitute the physical world. The other elements are Earth (Prithvi), Water (Jala), Air (Vayu), and Ether or Space (Akasha) which are described in the chapter related to Lalita Tripura Sundari.

Agni is revered as a deity and has both a physical and metaphysical presence. It is associated with heat, light, transformation, energy, and purification. Fire is seen as a purifying force that can cleanse impurities and offerings in rituals and ceremonies. Agni is invoked during religious ceremonies, such as Yajnas (sacrificial rituals) and Havans (fire rituals), where sacred offerings are made into the fire. The fire is believed to carry the offerings to the deities and act as a conduit between the physical and spiritual realms.

Symbolically, fire is also associated with knowledge, illumination, and spiritual awakening. It represents the flame of consciousness and the burning away of ignorance and attachment to achieve spiritual enlightenment.

Bhairavi is often addressed as Tripura Bhairavi, signifying that she resides in the three realms of existence, awareness, and eternal bliss. Tripura, in her context, also refers to her power and control over Agni (fire), Vidyut (lightening), and Surya (sunlight), as she is seen as the goddess of Tejastattva.

Tejas refers to the subtle essence of fire or radiance, representing the transformative and illuminating aspects of consciousness. Tejas is therefore closely associated with the Tanmatras, the building blocks of the physical world and the subtle essences of sensory experiences. They are the fundamental qualities that form the basis of our perception and are associated with the five senses: sound (Shabda), touch (Sparsha), form (Rupa), taste (Rasa), and smell (Gandha).

Both Tejas and Tanmatras are subtle forces that underlie the physical realm and play a significant role in the process of manifestation and experience. Bhairavi is therefore a goddess who governs our sensory experiences. She grants the capacity to control the senses, thoughts, and emotions completely, thereby making tapas possible. The term Tapas comes from the Sanskrit root "tapa," which means "to heat" or "to burn." It refers to the fiery inner discipline and intense effort to attain spiritual goals and transform themselves. Tapas is associated with austerity, penance, and self-control. It involves voluntary practices of discipline, such as fasting, meditation, prayer, celibacy, and rigorous physical or mental exercises. The purpose of tapas is to purify the body, mind, and soul, and to cultivate spiritual strength, willpower, and self-realization.

Through Tapas, individuals strive to transcend their physical and mental limitations, overcome desires and attachments, and attain higher levels of consciousness. Tapas generates spiritual energy and burns away impurities, leading to spiritual growth and union with the divine. Many legendary sages, ascetics, and yogis are depicted as engaging in rigorous tapas to attain enlightenment or gain supernatural powers. It is considered a vital aspect of the spiritual path.

Kavita Chinnaiyan writes: "In the process of creation, the first movement is that of desire, represented by Tripura Sundari, or Iccha shakti. The perception of this desire resulting in the space for creation to occur is symbolized by Bhuvaneshwari, or Jnana Shakti. The actualization of infinite divinity taking up finite forms by the process of energizing Itself in specific ways is depicted by Tripura Bhairavi, or Kriya shakti. This process is one of Tapas, which is immense concentration or self-awareness of the absolute, resulting in the transmutation of that force into energized action. In the Vedas, this self-awareness is equated with the light of consciousness that is aflame in every being, known as the "Chid-agni".

Since Bhairavi is associated with Tapas, she is also seen as the power behind Kundalini shakti. Kundalini literally means coiled serpent referring to the energy which lies dormant at the Muladhara Chakra, located at the base of the spine, from where it ascends towards the Sahasrara Chakra. According to Kundalini Yoga, the human body carries a subtle energy channel called the Sushumna, which moves upward, activating and aligning the various chakras along the way until it reaches the Sahasrara chakra, where profound spiritual transformation, expanded consciousness, and union with the divine take place.

Tripurabhairavi represents Para Vak, the supreme power of speech, which is closely related to Tejastattva. She is the word in its unarticulated and primal form as raw energy, where it appears like a burning weapon to remove all resistance. In Hindu philosophy, four aspects of speech are collectively known as "Vak", representing different dimensions of communication and speech, encompassing both verbal and non-verbal forms of expression. They are:

- Para Vak, which refers to the highest or transcendent aspect of speech. It represents the divine consciousness from which all speech originates. Para Vak is beyond the limitations of ordinary language and is associated with the cosmic sound or vibration that underlies creation.

- Pashyanti Vak is the stage of speech where thoughts and ideas begin to take form. It is the subtle level of speech where the speaker experiences a deep sense of inner awareness and conceptualization. Pashyanti Vak represents the stage of formulation and represents the bridge between the unmanifest and manifest aspects of speech.

- Madhyama Vak is the intermediate or transitional stage of speech. It is the level at which thoughts or concepts take on a more recognizable form, preparing to be expressed verbally. Madhyama Vak involves the mental process of structuring thoughts into words and sentences.

- Vaikhari Vak is the gross or physical manifestation of speech. It is the actual spoken or articulated speech that other people can hear and understand. Vaikhari Vak is the final stage where thoughts and ideas are expressed through words, sounds, and gestures, allowing communication to occur on an external level.

These four aspects of speech represent a continuum from the transcendent and subtle to the gross and physical, illustrating the process through which thoughts and ideas are transformed into meaningful communication.

In the Eastern and Northern Tantric Sampradayas, the term Bhairavi is used to describe an accomplished woman practitioner who has been given appropriate diksha and who is well versed in Shakti sadhana. The Vedanta Society, in an article on the Mahavidya, says that Bhairavi is also a title conferred upon a female devotee who has succeeded in learning the Kundalini Tantra. "A Bhairavi is one who has succeeded, who has achieved a state which is beyond the fear of death, and therefore awesome."

The worship of Tripurabhairavi is particularly popular among those who practice tapas in an effort to master their senses, emotions, and wandering thoughts (Brahmacharya). She provides support during various spiritual disciplines, such as fasting, vows of silence, meditation retreats, pilgrimages, and the practice of celibacy. Regardless of the challenges that may arise during Tapas, invoking Tripurabhairavi helps overcome these obstacles and impediments, allowing us to progress on our spiritual path with her guidance when she takes on the role of anugrahatmika, the giver of infinite grace.

Bhairavi can be accessed through the Panchamakaras, the five ritualistic elements used in Tantra. The Panchamakara are:

1. Madya representing the ritual consumption of alcohol

2. Mamsa representing the ritual consumption of meat

3. Matsya is the inclusion of fish or fish-related elements

4. Mudra is the use of grains or cereals

5. Maithuna representing the ritualistic sexual union between a male and female

In the Tantric context, the consumption of alcohol is a metaphorical inference to embracing the divine essence within oneself and all creation. Mamsa represents the acceptance and integration of the primal and instinctual aspects of human nature.

Symbolically, it emphasizes the breaking of societal taboos and transcending limitations to experience the divine in all forms. Matsya is associated with fertility, abundance, and the cosmic waters of creation. It signifies the flow of life force and the interconnectedness of all beings. Mudra relates to the importance of material sustenance and the integration of the physical and spiritual aspects of life. Maithuna is viewed as a sacred and transformative act that symbolizes the union of opposites, the merging of Shiva and Shakti energies, and the attainment of spiritual awakening and liberation.

Yogi Anand Saraswati writes: "The worship of Bhairavi using the Panchamakara rituals does not imply any Himsa (violence); it only suggests Ananda (bliss). In Madya, one gets drunk with the knowledge that there is no separate existence from the supreme power; in Mamsa, the worshipper offers himself to her divine grace; in Matsya, the devotee sees himself as a jiva floating in the paramatma; in Mudra, the devotee makes gestures that depict her prowess; and in Maithuna, the union that occurs is on a spiritual level using inner consciousness. Those who understand this essential oneness get liberated, and those who get entangled with the Tanmatras of Shabda, Sparsha, Rupa, Rasa, and Gandha remain deluded through the illusion of separateness."

Bhairavi can be worshipped through the Vedic sacrificial fire (Homa), or she can be accessed through subtle, inner worship by offering all the thoughts and emotions to the spiritual fire of Tapas. Inner worship can help cultivate a deep and personal relationship with the divine through meditation, prayer, chanting mantras, visualization, and introspection.

Bhairavi is seen as the presiding goddess of the Lagna house in the horoscope. In Vedic astrology, Lagna, also known as the Ascendant or the First House, is a crucial element in the birth chart. It represents the zodiac sign that was rising on the eastern horizon at the exact time and location of an individual's birth. Lagna is considered the most significant point in the birth chart, as it sets the foundation for the entire chart and plays a vital role in determining various aspects of one's life.

According to Vedic astrology, Lagna can offer insights into the physical appearance, mental outlook and overall personality of an individual. It influences how one presents oneself to the world and how others one is perceived by others. The Lagna also influences several other important factors, such as the planetary periods, Dasha and Bhukti, which are calculated based on the Lagna. These periods indicate the timing of various events and significant phases in a person's life. The Lagna determines the placement of the other houses in the birth chart. It helps determine the strength and significance of different areas of life, such as career, relationships, finances, and health. Lagna is considered important in determining auspicious timings for various activities, such as starting a new venture, performing rituals, or making important decisions. Bhairavi is invoked for Lagna-shuddhi, to protect and purify the defects of the horoscope.

Bhairavi's fierceness is directed at the destruction of impurities and the elimination of negative forces. Her energy, which has a terrible, fear-inspiring aspect, burns down those aspects that threaten to keep her devotees from achieving their spiritual goals. Her action is compared to a mother's righteous anger, which is aroused when she has to defend her child from any external threat. A mother is compelled to take immediate, determined steps to safeguard her offspring in much the same way that Bhairavi takes instantaneous actions to protect her devotees.

Chhinnamasta – The Selfless Friend

ॐ

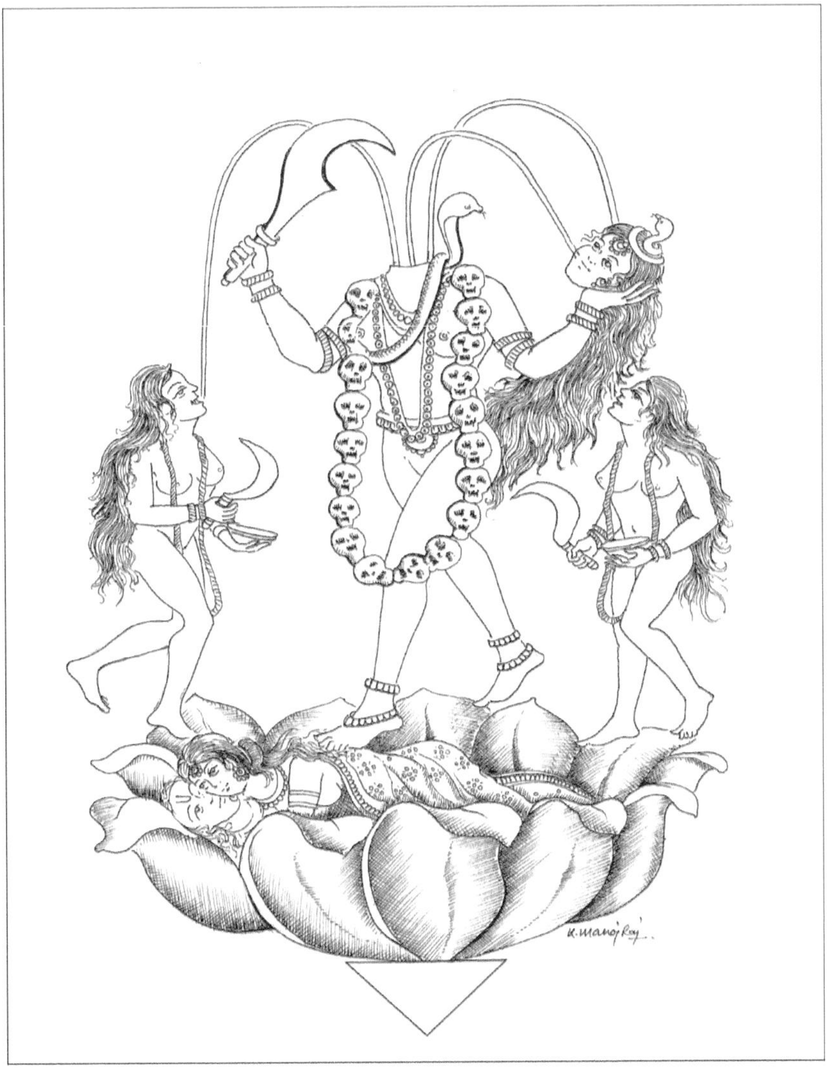

Pratyalida padaam sadaiva dadhatim chhinam shirah kartrakam
Dig vastram sva kabandha shonita sudha dharam pibantim muda
Naga abadha shiro manim trinayanam hridya utpala alangkritam
Ratyasakta mano-bhavopari dridham dhyayet japa sannibham

I meditate on Devi Chhinnamasta
Who stands with her left foot extended forward and her right foot drawn back
And always holding a severed head and a sword
Who is clothed by the directions, and whose severed head is joyfully drinking The nectar of blood flowing down from her own headless trunk
Who wears a gem on her head, bound by a serpent
Who has three eyes and whose heart is adorned with a lotus
Who is firmly standing above the tendencies of the mind to love the attachments of the world
Who is to be meditated upon as having the bright red colour of the hibiscus

Even in the Tantric pantheon of the Mahavidya, which encompasses some of the most fierce and terrifying forms found in any global religious tradition, the iconography of Goddess Chhinnamasta stands out as the most distinct, striking, and unforgettable image. Here is a goddess who cuts off her own head while standing naked on a copulating couple and has three streams of blood oozing out of her decapitated neck, two streams flowing into the mouths of her hungry friends, and one stream of blood being consumed by herself. On account of this gruesome imagery, the Tantrasara calls her Prachanda Chandika. Chandi herself is a fierce form, but Chhinnamasta is even more fierce.

The word Chhinnamasta is made up of two Sanskrit words, Chhinna and Masta. The word Chhinna means severed, and Masta means the head. Therefore, Chhinnamasta means "the one with a severed head".

One legend attributed to the Narada Pancharatna, tells the story of Parvati and her two female attendants, Dakini and Varnini, bathing in the Mandakini river. Dakini and Varnini become extremely hungry and beg Parvati to get some food for them. Parvati promises to give them food once they return home, but they insist that their hunger is unbearable. Parvati, as the mother of the world, cannot deny them food and so beheads herself using a scimitar, places it on the palm of her left hand, and offers them her blood to satisfy their hunger.

The Pranatoshini Tantra suggests that during the Samudra Manthan (the churning of the oceans), which threw up both nectar and poison, Chhinnamasta drank the Asuras' share of elixir (which would have given them immortality) and then decapitated herself to prevent them from acquiring it, thereby allowing the Devatas to continue their righteous reign over the worlds.

Chhinnamasta is described in the Trishakti Tantra and the Tantrasara (Prachandachandika section) most evocatively as having a red complexion akin to a hibiscus flower and appearing as bright as a million suns. She is naked, with her private parts hidden with jewellery and a multi-hooded cobra coiled around her waist. She is shown with two hands. Though no legend mentions a specific weapon for the beheading, she holds a scimitar or a scissor-like object in her right hand. She carries her own severed head in her left hand.

Both the attendants, Dakini to her left and Varnini to her right, are depicted nude, with matted or dishevelled hair, three-eyed, full-breasted, wearing the serpentine sacred thread, the skull necklace, and carrying the skull-bowl in the left hand and the knife in the right.

She adopts the Pratyalidha pose, a posture in which the right foot is bent and the left foot is put forward as she stands on top of Kama and his wife Rati, who are engaged in copulation. Below the couple is a lotus with an inverted triangle, and in the background is a cremation ground.

The head is the most unique mark of identity, and self-decapitation therefore represents the removal of Maya (illusion or delusion associated with one's identity). Chhinnamasta allows the devotee to gain a consciousness that transcends the bonds of physical attachment, the body, and the mind through her self-sacrifice. The ability to remain alive despite the beheading is associated with supernatural powers and the awakening of the kundalini, which we first came across in association with Bhairavi. By severing her own head and transcending the limitations of the physical body, she demonstrates the potential for radical transformation and rebirth. Chhinnamasta teaches that true liberation lies in the dissolution of the false self and the awakening to the eternal and infinite nature of the soul.

Chhinnamasta is depicted in a naked form, representing the state of non-duality and the absence of worldly attachments. Her nakedness signifies the shedding of all illusions and the embrace of the unadorned truth. Through the consumption of her own blood, Chhinnamasta represents the realization of non-duality and the unity of all existence. She teaches that divine energy permeates all aspects of creation and that the external world is a manifestation of the same divine essence that resides within us.

The couple engaged in copulation on whom Chhinamasta stands symbolize life and the urge to create life. The inverted triangle, which is also an important aspect of her yantra, signifies the *yoni* (womb). Chhinnamasta, through this imagery, signifies that life, death, and sex are interdependent, conveying the eternal truth that life feeds on death, is nourished by death, necessitates death, and that the ultimate destiny of sex is to perpetuate more life, which in turn will decay and die in order to feed more life.

The scholar Van Kooij notes that the iconography of Chhinnamasta has elements of heroism (vira rasa) and terror (bhayanaka rasa) as well as eroticism (sringara rasa) as seen in the image of the copulating couple. The main motifs in her iconography are the offering of her own severed head, the spilling and drinking of blood, and the trampling of the couple.

Chhinnamasta is seen as a figure of radical transformation, conveying the universal message that all life is sustained by other forms of life, and that destruction and sacrifice are necessary for the continuity of creation. She symbolizes pralaya (cosmic dissolution), where she swallows all creation and makes way for new creation, thus conveying the idea of transformation.

Elizabeth Anne Bernard writes that Chhinnamasta is a goddess of contradictions: she "is both the food and the eater of food, thereby symbolizing the whole world by this act of being devoured and the devourer. The dichotomy of receiver and giver, or object and subject, collapses into one." Her sahasranama (thousand name-hymn) echoes paradoxes; she is Prachanda Chandika (the powerfully fierce one) as well as Sarvanandapradayini (the prime giver of all Ananda or bliss).

Her names convey the idea that, though she is fierce at first appearance, she can be gentle to those who worship her.

Some of the other contradictions that Chhinnamasta stands for are that she is both a life-taker (even if the life she takes is her own) and a life-giver (as she nourishes her friends with her own blood). She is considered both a symbol of sexual self-control and an embodiment of sexual energy. She represents death, temporality, and destruction as well as life, immortality, and recreation.

While other fierce Hindu goddesses like Kali depict severing the heads of demons, Chhinnamasta's motif reverses the ritual head-offering, offering her own head to the attendants in order to feed them. She symbolizes the aspect of Shakti as a giver, much like Annapurna, the goddess of food, and Shakambhari, the goddess of vegetables. Mary Storm, writes in Head and Heart: Valour and Self-Sacrifice in the Art of India that the element of self-sacrifice is the symbol of "divine reciprocation" by the deity to her devotees.

Pratapaditya Pal, an expert on South Asian art, equates Chhinnamasta with the concept of sacrifice necessary to renew creation. She sacrifices herself, and her blood, drunk by her attendants, is analogous to her sacrifice nourishing all that is hungry and needs nourishment in the universe. One invocation calls her the sacrifice, the sacrificer, and the recipient of the sacrifice, with the severed head seen as an offering. This is only one of the many paradoxes that Chhinnamasta's imagery evokes, he adds.

Chhinnamasta represents the awakening of the Kundalini which begins in the Muladhara chakra with the copulating couple symbolising this arousal. The Kundalini energy flows through the Sushumna nadi and hits the Sahasrara chakra at the top of her head with immense force, thereby causing her head to be separated from the body. The blood spilling out from the throat represents the upward-flowing kundalini, breaking all knots (<u>granthis</u>) along the way. The serpent in her iconography is also a symbol of the Kundalini. Other interpretations associate Daknini, Varnini, and Chhinnamasta with the three main nadis: Ida, Pingala, and Sushumna, respectively.

Chhinnamasta is associated with thunder and lightning. Her epithet, Vajra Vairochani (radiant like the vajra), is linked to the Vajra (thunderbolt). In various Hindu scriptures such as Vedanta and Samkhya, the creation of the universe is described as having occurred in stages, and the concepts of Prakasha and Nada play significant roles in this cosmological understanding. Prakasha refers to light or illumination, while nada refers to sound or vibration. These two principles are considered fundamental aspects of creation.

Prakasha represents the illuminating aspect of Brahman. It signifies consciousness, knowledge, and awareness. It is the divine light that brings forth the potential for creation. In the context of the creation process, Prakasha represents the subtlest form of energy or cosmic intelligence that permeates all existence. Nada represents the vibratory aspect of Brahman. It symbolizes the creative force or energy that gives rise to the manifestation of the universe. Nada is associated with "Om", the primordial sound of creation, which is the source of all other sounds and forms in the universe.

The interplay between Prakasha and Nada sets in motion the process of creation. The subtle vibrations of Nada interact with the cosmic intelligence of Prakasha, leading to the formation of the material universe. It is through the dynamic interplay of light and sound that the cosmos, with all its diversity and complexity, comes into being.

There are two contrasting interpretations of Chhinnamasta with regard to sexual desire. Some scholars interpret the image of Chhinnamasta standing on a mating pair of Kama and Rati as a symbol of a person's control over sexual desire, while others see the goddess as the embodiment of sexual energy. Her names, such as Madanatura (one who has control of Kama), convey her control over sexual energy. Her stance with the couple under her foot signifies victory over desire.

We use the term "losing one's head" as an idiomatic expression to convey the idea of losing control, composure, or rationality in a given situation. It is used metaphorically rather than literally, referring to the physical act of decapitation. When someone "loses their head," it implies that they are overwhelmed by emotions or circumstances, leading them to behave impulsively or irrationally. They may become angry, frustrated, or panic to the point where they are unable to think clearly or make rational decisions. It can also suggest a loss of self-control, where one's actions or words become reckless or out of character.

The origin of the term losing one's head likely stems from the dramatic imagery of a beheading, which represents a severe and irreversible loss. Losing one's head metaphorically implies a similar loss—of reason, judgment, or emotional stability. The fear that arises from losing one's head is largely that of a temporary loss of identity, but for those on the spiritual path, the absence of a head is a reference to the transcendence of one's own identification with the illusion of self and points to a dissolution of attachments, ideas, and habits of the mind.

The concept of "losing one's head" can easily be understood without relying on a dramatic image like that of Chhinnamasta. However, visual images tend to have a more profound and immediate impact on the subconscious mind, leading to quicker and more powerful shifts in our understanding and behaviour. They can create a more significant and transformative effect compared to a purely theoretical explanation.

Chhinnamasta embodies a striking visual representation that symbolizes the profound transformation of an individual. It signifies the relinquishment of the limited and transient egoic self, allowing one to merge ecstatically into the boundless Universal Consciousness. Importantly, the expression on Chhinnamasta's decapitated head does not convey suffering or pain; instead, it reflects the blissful state of contentment and peace.

The significance of this aspect lies in the joy of transcending earthly limitations and the suffering caused by attachment to them. Despite the severed head, it does not appear lifeless; in fact, it exudes even greater vitality. This signifies that consciousness is not confined to the dimensions and functions of the physical body but exists independently.

Chhinnamasta symbolically consumes the blood, representing the joys, sufferings, pains, and hopes of earthly life. In doing so, she absorbs and transmutes the fragmented experiences of time, including disappointments and illusions, into a higher state of being.

In Hinduism, it is believed that the atman leaves the physical body through one of the nine orifices. The souls of those who have lived a spiritual life will exit through the Brahmarandhra, located at the top of the head (specifically at the crown or fontanelle region), and attain moksha. Those with more profane attachments will leave through the other orifices and continue on the karmic cycle of birth and death, based on the extent of their spiritual evolution. The Sahasrara, or crown chakra, associated with the Brahmarandhra, is considered the highest and most significant of these energy centres.

The Brahmarandhra is depicted as a subtle gateway through which divine energy can enter or exit the body. It is associated with higher consciousness, spiritual awakening, and the union of the individual self (Atman) with the ultimate reality (Brahman). Activation and balancing of the crown chakra are believed to facilitate spiritual growth, expanded awareness, and a sense of transcendence.

In yogic practices such as Kundalini yoga and meditation, attention and focus is directed towards the Brahmarandhra to awaken and activate the crown chakra. This can involve various techniques, including visualization, breathwork, and mantra chanting, to encourage the flow of energy and attain higher states of consciousness.

Chhinnamasta, the headless goddess, embodies the profound paradoxes of existence. She symbolizes the transformative power of sacrifice and the liberation found in the dissolution of the ego. Through her terrifying image, she invites us to transcend the limited self and merge with the infinite consciousness of the divine.

Dhumavati – The Jealous Widow

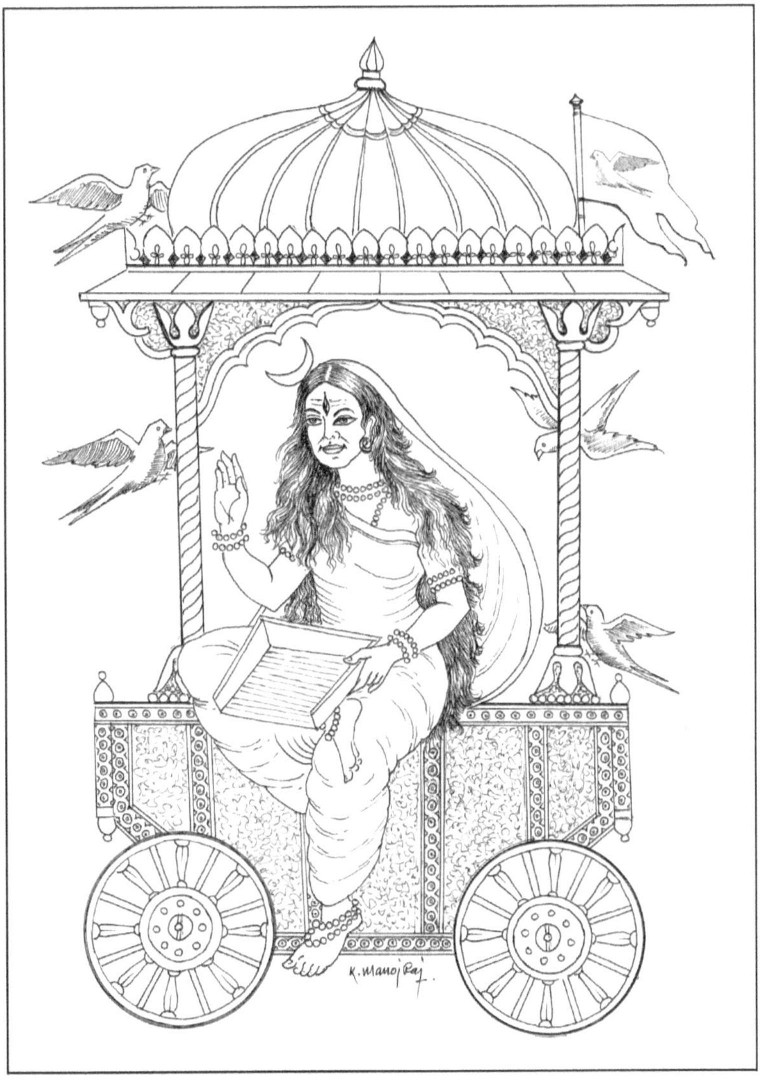

Vivarna chanchala rusta dirgha cha malina-ambara
Vivarna kuntala ruksha vidhava virala-dvija
Kaaka dhvaja ratha rudha vilambita payodhara
Shurpa hasta ati ruksha aksi dhrita hasta varanvita
Pravridha ghona tu bhrisham kuttila kuttileksana
ksut-pipasardita nityam bhayada kalaha-priya

I meditate on Devi Dhumavati who is pale in appearance
Restless and always irritated, large in stature and wearing pale clothes
Whose locks of hair are unkempt, her skin dry and rough
Who is a widow with sparse teeth
Whose flag has the symbol of a crow
Who is mounted on a chariot and whose breasts are hanging down
Who is holding a winnowing basket in Her hand
Whose eyes are very rough and harsh
Who is showing the varada mudra with her hand
Who is very old
Whose nose and eyes are excessively crooked
Who is always afflicted by hunger and thirst
Whose appearance incites fear
She is always intent upon picking up a quarrel

Lalita Tripurasundari and Bhuvaneswari depict the most beautiful stages in a woman's life as they enjoy the excitement, vibrancy, and attention that accompanies youth and beauty. Dhumavati serves as a vivid reminder that youth and beauty are both short-lived, and a time will come in everyone's life when old age, loneliness, and disease will be the predominant motifs. This stage is not without its positive attributes, as it is fertile ground for pursuing the spiritual path, as social obligations and worldly desires are all now in the past and one is focused on a future dedicated to spiritual upliftment and the unilateral pursuit of moksha.

The term Dhumavati means the smokey one, as "dhuma" means smoke or haze. A legend from the Shaktisamgama-Tantra describes that Sati commited suicide by jumping in Daksha's yagna, and Dhumavati rose with a grayish face from the smoke of Sati's burning body. She is a crone, an ancestor or Grandmother spirit, and her smokey appearance hides that which is obvious, revealing hidden secrets and truths of the unknown and the unmanifest upon deeper study and introspection.

The origin story of Dhumavati can be found in the Pranatosini Tantra. Sati once felt extreme hunger and asked Shiva to bring her something to eat. Shiva refused, saying that he was not a householder and hence it was not his duty to satisfy her hunger. Her repeated requests go unheeded, and in a fit of rage, she devoured Shiva, who, in his anger at being eaten, cursed her. He cursed that she would be a widow and go through all the heartache, pain, and sorrow that follow. Sati heard this curse, and her beauty became enveloped in smoke. She became ugly, lonely, and frustrated. Now separated from her husband, she lived a solitary existence on the cremation grounds with only the crow for company.

The Dhumavati Tantra describes her as an old and ugly widow with a wrinkled, angry face and a cloud-like complexion. She is thin, tall, unhealthy, wears old, dirty clothes, and has dishevelled hair. Her eyes are fearsome, her nose long and crooked, and some of her long fang-like teeth have fallen out, leaving her smile with gaps. She wears no jewellery. In one of her hands, she holds a winnowing basket, while the other is in the varada mudra (boon-giving gesture) or chinmudra (knowledge-giving gesture). She sits in the cremation grounds atop a horseless chariot, hoisting a banner that has the emblem of a crow.

Dhumavati's portrayal as a widow points to a feminine principle devoid of the support of a masculine element. She is the only one of the Mahavidya without a consort. She sits on a stalled, horseless chariot, showing that she has nowhere to go in life and society. The crow, as an eater of carrion, symbolizes death. It is a fitting companion for a goddess of misfortune. Another motif linking her with death is the presence of a cremation ground and pyres in the background. Her sahasranama (thousand-name hymn) says that she lives in the cremation ground, sits on a corpse, wears ashes, and blesses those who haunt the grounds. The winnowing basket that she carries in one hand is used to separate the chaff from the grain. It is symbolic of Viveka, the mental discrimination between the permanent and the fleeting, and points to the need to separate the outer illusory form from the inner reality.

Dhumavati has no independent existence outside the Mahavidya group. There are no temples specially dedicated to her worship, and there is no historical mention of her before her association with the Mahavidya. Tantra experts point out that Dhumavati's antecedents can be linked with three Vedic goddesses -Nirriti, Jyeshta, and Alakshmi. In Vedic mythology, Nirriti is a goddess associated with destruction, chaos, and misfortune. She is depicted as a fearsome deity who brings calamity, hardship, and discord. Nirriti is considered to be one of the adhi-devatas (primary deities) responsible for maintaining the cosmic order.

While Nirriti represents the destructive aspects of existence, she is acknowledged as an inherent part of the overall balance and functioning of the universe. Her presence serves as a reminder of the transient and impermanent nature of life.

Jyestha is a goddess mentioned in the Rigveda, symbolizing elderhood, superiority, and seniority. Jyestha is considered to be the elder sister of Lakshmi, the goddess of wealth and prosperity, and is sometimes regarded as her contrasting or shadow aspect. In some interpretations, Jyestha represents the path of renunciation and austerity, in contrast to Lakshmi's association with material abundance. Alakshmi is considered the opposite of Lakshmi and is associated with inauspiciousness, poverty, and misfortune. Alakshmi can disrupt or diminish prosperity and abundance. She is believed to bring obstacles, financial difficulties, and disharmony into people's lives. However, she is also regarded as a reminder of the cyclical nature of fortune and the need for balance in life. Worship or propitiation of Alakshmi is sometimes performed to appease her negative influence and seek the blessings of Lakshmi.

Like Nirriti, Dhumavati represents the negative, unfortunate aspects of existence; like Jyeshta, she brings about quarrels, inhabits inauspicious places, and has a foul temperament; and like Alakshmi, she can diminish prosperity and abundance. Dhumavati is therefore associated with all that is unlucky, unattractive, and inauspicious. She rules over Chaturmas, a period of four months in the Hindu calendar that occurs during the monsoon season. Chaturmas begins in the Hindu month of Ashadha (June or July) and ends in the month of Kartik (October or November). It is believed that during this period, Lord Vishnu, the preserver of the universe, goes into a state of deep slumber. As a result, it is considered an inauspicious time for certain activities and celebrations. Observing Chaturmas is seen as an opportunity for devotees to intensify their spiritual practices and engage in acts of devotion, austerity, and self-restraint.

The Pranatosinitantra, when classifying the Mahavidya based on guna, associates her with tamas, signifying ignorance and darkness. Dhumavati is said to manifest at the time of pralaya (cosmic dissolution) and is seen as "the void" that exists before creation and after dissolution. Vedic scholar Ganapati Muni describes her thus in the Uma Sahasram:

"Perceived as the Void, as the dissolved form of consciousness, when all beings are dissolved in sleep in the supreme Brahman, having swallowed the entire universe, the seer-poets call her the most glorious and the eldest, Dhumavati. She exists in the forms of sleep, lack of memory, illusion, and dullness in the creatures immersed in the illusion of the world, but among the yogis she becomes the power that destroys all thoughts, indeed Samadhi (death and liberation) itself."

In traditional Indian society, becoming a widow is seen as the biggest stroke of misfortune, a fate worse than death. A woman, devoid of the support of her husband, is marginalized and left at the periphery of society, unwelcome at auspicious events such as marriages and housewarming ceremonies. Her position, now relegated to an unimportant post in the household, is, in a way, an involuntary imposition of sanyasa (a renunciation of the world). She is now free to pursue her path as she finds herself free of familial and societal obligations. She is now free, if she so desires, to walk on the path of spiritual development. In this sense, Dhumavati is a symbol of how misfortune can be turned into positive aspects of personal growth, resilience, and the pursuit of wisdom.

Misfortune often presents us with challenges and obstacles that force us to reassess our beliefs, values, and priorities and give us a deeper appreciation for the positive aspects of life that we may have taken for granted. Going through difficult times can enhance our capacity for empathy and compassion towards others who are facing similar challenges. It can deepen our understanding of human suffering and motivate us to support and uplift those in need. Misfortune can prompt us to re-evaluate our life choices, priorities, and direction. It can be an opportunity for introspection and self-reflection, leading us to make necessary course corrections or pursue new paths that align with our authentic selves and values.

This is why Dhumavati, in spite of her inauspicious qualities, is bestowed with several positive aspects in her sahasranama (thousand-name hymn). She is described as a bestower of boons and a great teacher who reveals the ultimate knowledge of the universe. David Kinsley says: "Beyond name and form, beyond human categories, alone and indivisible, as the great dissolution, Dhumavati reveals the nature of ultimate knowledge, which is formless and knows no divisions into good or bad, pure and impure, auspicious and inauspicious.

David Frawley says, "Dhumavati shows the feminine principle of negation in all of its aspects. On an outer level, she represents poverty, destitution, and suffering—the great misfortunes that we all fear in life. Hence, she is said to be crooked, troublesome, and quarrelsome—a witch or a hag. Yet on an inner level, this same negativity causes us to seek a greater fulfilment that cannot be achieved in the limited realms of manifest creation. After all, only frustration in our outer lives causes us to seek our inner reality. Dhumavati is whatever obstructs us in life, but what obstructs us in one area can release a new potential to grow in a different direction. Thus, she is the good fortune that comes to us in the form of misfortune. Dhumavati represents the darkness on the face of the deep, the original chaos and obscurity that underlie creation. She is the darkness of primordial ignorance, Mulavidya, from which this world of illusion has arisen, and which it is seeking to transcend."

Dhumavati takes us into the limitless themes of the past, portraying the disappointments, frustration, sorrow, and loneliness that a woman endures in her old age. She also stands for knowledge that comes with experience and the understanding that what are initially perceived as unbearable hardships eventually reveal themselves to have a redemptive quality, which takes us many steps towards spiritual liberation. She is associated with Ketu, the planet of the past and the ancestors.

The broader lessons that Dhumavati can impart are many. The unpleasant experiences of life will cause us to feel a sense of disgust and turn us toward a search for the divine. The divine that we so desperately seek through various means is present everywhere, even in what we call ugly and unattractive things. We cannot remain confined to our past memories of youth, beauty, and well-being. Misfortune brings about the most important transformation necessary for us to grow as spiritual beings. Time will bring about change for everyone, and it is inevitably bound to lead to decay and death. We will all be slowly robbed of our beauty, youth, vigour, power, success, and good health as the years pass. One day, we will also be old, alone, and ugly, just like Dhumavati, sitting on a metaphorical cart that can no longer move. We too, like her, will eventually need to use the winnowing basket to discern reality from illusion using Viveka, our own power of discrimination, and reach towards the ultimate goal of liberation.

Bagalamukhi – The Paralyser of Enemies

ॐ

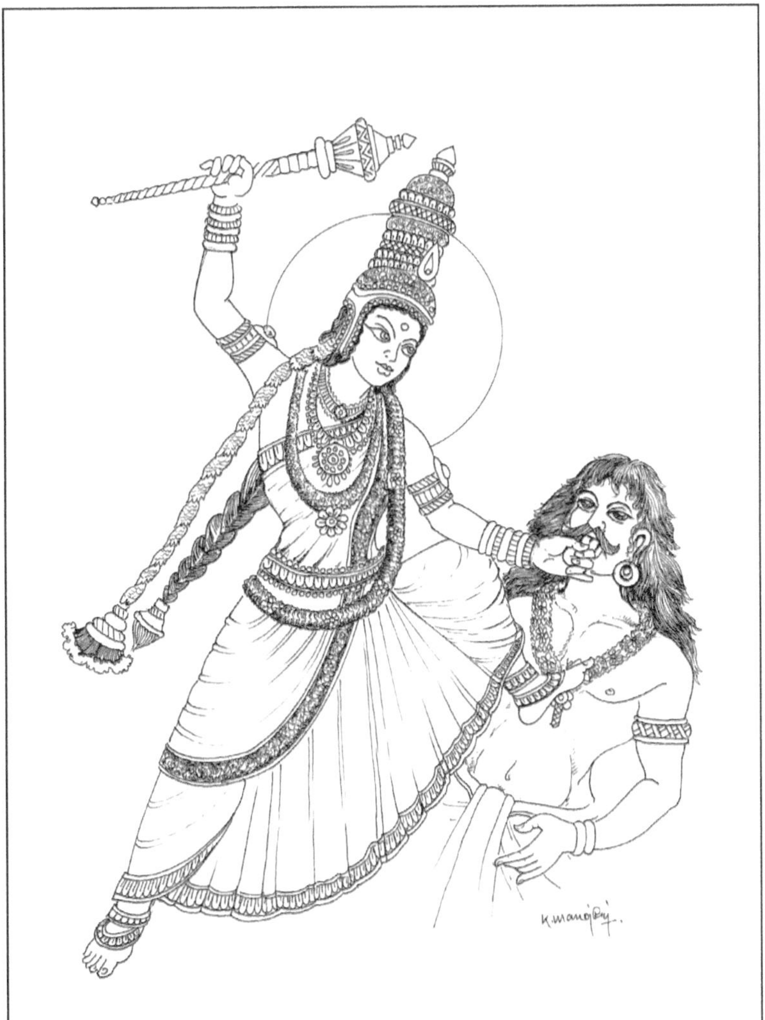

Madhye sudhabdhi mani mandapa ratna vedyam
Simhasanoupari gatam paripita varnam
Pitambara abharana malya vibhusita angim
Devim smarami dhirta mudgara vairi jihvam
Jihvagram adaya karena devim vamena shatrun paripidayantim
Gada abhighatena ca dakshinena pitambaradhyam dvi bhujam
namami

I meditate on Devi Bagalamukhi
Seated in the middle of the ocean of nectar, on a platform studded
with gems
She has a yellow complexion
She is wearing yellow garments and adorned with garlands and
ornaments,
I remember the form of Devi and meditate on her
Who is holding a mallet
Who is holding the tip of the tongue of the enemy with her
left hand
And striking him with mace with her right hand
I salute the two-armed Devi who is richly
decorated with yellow garments

Tantra is a vast and diverse spiritual tradition that encompasses a wide range of practices, philosophies, and rituals. Tantra includes both Vamachara (left-hand) and Dakshinachara (right-hand) paths, each with its own methodologies and goals. Vamachara is associated with "black rites", techniques that may seem unconventional, transgressive, or controversial compared to mainstream societal norms. It is crucial to understand that the concept of "black" does not imply inherently negative or malevolent intentions. One such black practice is called Stambhana, meant to arrest the movements of an opponent, thereby instantly stopping him from carrying out harmful actions. Bagalamukhi, according to Ganapati Muni, holds this Stambhana Shakti, which includes being armed with the Brahmastra as her ultimate weapon.

According to etymology experts, the word Bagalamukhi arises out of the corruption of the word Valga which comes from the term Balaka in Sanskrit. Balaka refers to the crane and David Kinsley translates Bagalamukhi as "she who has the face of a crane" even though she is rarely depicted with a crane-head or seen with cranes in her iconography. He points out that her association with this aquatic bird is symbolic of a crane's behavior as it stands perfectly still to catch its prey. The crane is a reflection of the occult power of Sthambana bestowed by the goddess.

Valga also means a bridle (placed in the mouth to guide a horse) and Mukhi means face. Other experts define Bagalamukhi as a name that stands for the one "whose face has the power to control or conquer". She is known by the popular epithet Pitambaradevi or Pitambari, "one who wears yellow clothes".

Her origin story can be found in the Tantrasara. In the first epoch in Hindu cosmology, known as Satya Yuga, a great cosmic storm appeared, throwing the world into turbulence and fear. Vishnu, the God of Sustenance, was perturbed as he did not know how to control the storm. He performed austerities and meditated to appease the goddess Parvati on the shore of the Haridra Sarovar, the lake of turmeric. The goddess appeared in her manifestation as Bagalamukhi and calmed the storm using the magic of *Stambhana* to restore order to the universe.

Another story tells of a demon called Madan who acquires the power of vak siddhi, the ability to make whatever he utters come true. The Gods seek Bagalamukhi's help as Madan goes berserk with his newly acquired power. She uses the magic of Stambhana and gets hold of his tongue, thereby preventing him from speaking. She lifts her club to slay him but grants his wish to always be seen whenever the Goddess is depicted in her name form. Her iconography shows a defeated Madan praying at her feet as she holds his tongue with one hand.

The Tantrasara describes her as sitting on a golden throne decorated with purple lotus flowers in the midst of an ocean. Her complexion is golden yellow. She wears yellow clothes, a garland of yellow champaka flowers, and is bedecked with gold ornaments. She holds the tongue of the demon Madan in her left hand, while her right hand is raised to strike him with a club. A yellow half-moon adorns her forehead. In some texts, she is described as having the head of a crane or seen riding a crane as her vahana.

Yellow is obtained from the roots of turmeric, which holds great importance in Hindu rituals and ceremonies. It is considered a sacred herb and is associated with auspiciousness and divine blessings. It is believed to possess purifying properties, both on a physical and spiritual level. Turmeric plays a significant role in Hindu wedding and marriage rituals. It is a common practice to apply turmeric paste, known as Haldi, to the bride and groom during pre-wedding ceremonies. This is believed to enhance their beauty, purify them, and bless them with a prosperous married life. Bagalamukhi's dhyana mantras urge her devotees to wear yellow while worshiping her and to employ a mala made of turmeric beads. Yellow is also the colour of the sun, representing the light of consciousness.

The image of Bagalamukhi holding the tongue of the demon is symbolic of her absolute control over speech, as she can abruptly put a stop to it. In the yogic traditions, it is emphasized that the negative force of the ego manifests most prominently through speech. This concept is rooted in the understanding that the ego tends to assert itself and create divisions thereby reinforcing a sense of separateness which is done mainly through communication. When we speak, we express our thoughts, opinions, and personal perspectives. The ego, seeking validation and recognition, tends to identify strongly with these expressions, further reinforcing its sense of individuality. This identification can lead to arguments, conflicts, and an illusion of separateness.

Speech is often a response to external stimuli or internal thoughts and emotions. The ego, being reactive in nature, gets triggered easily and expresses itself through impulsive, defensive, or aggressive speech. Unconscious and unchecked speech can perpetuate negative emotions, conflicts, and disharmony.

Recognizing the role of speech in ego manifestation, spiritual practices often emphasize the importance of mindful and conscious communication. Practices like self-reflection, cultivating awareness, and practicing non-violent communication (ahimsa) can help us become more conscious of speech and reduce aggressive expressions. By observing our speech patterns, listening attentively, choosing words wisely, and speaking with empathy and compassion, we can work towards aligning our communication with higher virtues and fostering harmony, understanding, and connection with others.

Bagalamukhi is also known as Shatrubuddhivinashini or the destroyer of the enemy's mind. Most often, our greatest enemy is our own mind. She uses Stambhana as a power to annihilate the forces that oppose our spiritual evolution, which consist of all the thoughts, ideas, and feelings that arise from our mind and from our false identification with the concept of self. Manblunder, in his blog on Bagalamukhi, writes: "She smashes the arrogance of the enemies with her cudgel and silences them completely (removes our ego and silences our speech and thoughts, with uniform breath). Her act of holding the tongue, is to subdue the enemies from uttering anything against us."

She is also known as the Brahmastra Roopini, the form of Brahma's most powerful weapon. According to legend, Lord Brahma created and bestowed the Brahmastra upon divine beings and powerful warriors who sought his grace. Its creation involved intense penance and deep knowledge of sacred mantras and rituals. The Brahmastra is a powerful weapon capable of causing immense destruction and devastation and believed to possess the unique characteristic of selective targeting. It could be aimed at a specific individual, sparing others in the vicinity. Once the Brahmastra is invoked and released, its effects are irreversible, and there is no known way to stop or retract it, just as speech, once uttered, cannot be reversed, and the consequences will have to be borne by the speaker.

As Brahmastra Roopini, she can also be seen as the one who wields the ultimate weapon of spiritual knowledge. She paralyzes us into a stillness that leads us to ask the question, "Who am I?" This question seeks to transcend identification with the temporary aspects of our existence, such as the body, mind, and ego, and explore the deeper essence of our being. It invites us to inquire into their true nature beyond the limitations of the material world and the conditioned sense of self. This quest involves Atma Vichara (Self-Inquiry) as we turn our attention inward, seeking to discern the eternal essence beyond the changing aspects of existence. By stilling the mind through meditation, we can transcend our limited sense of self and experience a direct connection with the deeper truth of our being.

Swami Sarvapriyananda says, "Who am I?" has been a question, or rather, a quest, through the ages of human civilization that no material accumulation could satiate. Man's search for himself continues to this day, in order to find an answer to everything that he or she is a part of, whether awake or in dream. The seventh verse of the Mandukya Upanishad defines this I, or the self, as one beyond all three states: awake, dreaming, and deep sleep. The Self is the Turiya (Fourth), manifested through all the three states.

In the tantric tradition, Bagalamukhi is associated with Yoga as its practice involves Sthambana brought about by asanas, pranayama, and meditation. Asana involves maintaining a steady and balanced position, focusing on proper alignment, and holding the posture with stability and ease. Through breath control and meditation, yoga practitioners cultivate Sthambana, developing strength, concentration, and a deeper sense of presence.

Bagalamukhi 's power, according to Tantra texts, lies in the Talu (soft palate), located at the roof of the mouth, above the tongue. This is an important location as the vital sense organs of hearing, smelling, and tasting are closely placed, and it is considered a subtle energy centre, known as the Lalana chakra. A steady focus on the Talu, especially through the Khechari mudra by curling the tip of the tongue back into the mouth until it reaches above the soft palate, is believed to awaken spiritual energies in the body. According to Swami Kriyananda, "the assumption of this mudra helps to hasten the advent of deep spiritual states of consciousness."

In the Bagalamukhistotratram, a part of 'Rudrayamala', there is a hymn in praise of the her powers:

Vadi mukati rankati kshitipatirvaishwanarah sheetati krodhi
samyati durjanah Sujanati khsipranugah khanjati garvi khanjati
sarvaviccha jarati Tvanmantrinaamantritah srinitye baglamukhi
pratidinam tubhyam namah

By the effect of your mantra, good conversationalists become speechless; rich people become beggars; devastating fire gets cooled. The anger of the angry person is removed; an evil-minded person becomes good. The quick-moving person becomes crippled. The conceit of the arrogant is reduced. A knowledgeable person nearly becomes a fool. Salutations to the compassionate Bagalamukhi.

Julie Peters writes in an article titled Bagalamukhi the Paralyzer and How Stillness Moves Us Forward: "Bagalamukhi enters our lives when we need to slow down and shut up. When we speed through the day, telling anyone who will listen how busy we are, we don't have time to feel our feelings. This is often when we get sick or injured, as if our bodies are nailing our tongues to the ground for us. Alternatively, when we are stuck in the same routine, obsessing inside our repeating mental storms, Bagalamukhi asks us to move our bodies, to get outside, to change something. Stillness and movement work in relationship to each other, and in balance, they can help us sense what we deeply desire, what's gotten us stuck, or how we might want to change. Then we have the power to do something about it. That's Stambhana: the galvanizing power of Bagalamukhi the Paralyzer."

Matangi – The Outcaste Mother

Shyama angim shashi shekharam

Trinayanam ratna simhasana sthitam
Vedaih bahu dandair asi khetaka pasha angkusha dharam

I meditate on Devi Matangi whose complexion is dark blue

Who has the moon on her head

Who has three eyes and who is abiding on a throne which is
studded with gems
With her four arms she holds a sword, a shield, a noose and
a hook

Matangi, like the previous energy forms of Bhairavi and Bagalamukhi, is not very well known outside the circle of devout Tantra practitioners. She appears in various forms across the Indian subcontinent, seen as the daughter of the Elephant-King Matang in the North and as Madurai Meenakshi in the South. She is seen as the tantric, mystical, and occult form of Saraswati, the goddess of wisdom, music, and learning. Paradoxically, she is also associated with pollution and inauspiciousness, as embodied in one of her other manifestations, Uchchhishta Matangini.

The *Svatantra Tantra* tells the story of Sage Matanga, who practiced austerity for thousands of years to gain the power to subdue all beings. Lalita Tripura Sundari appeared to help fulfil his desires and blessed him with a daughter, whom he named Matangi. The Shaktisamgama-tantra narrates the tale of the birth of Uchchhishta Matangini. Vishnu and Lakshmi visited Shiva and his wife Parvati who, as hosts, offered all the gods a vast array of food. The deities dropped some food on the ground, from which arose a beautiful maiden, a manifestation of Goddess Saraswati, who asked for their leftovers. The deities granted her their leftovers as "prasada," which means favour or grace, as a divine gift. She asked Shiva for a boon to be worshipped as a goddess who could fulfil the material desires of her devotees. Shiva declared her the giver of boons while stating that those who repeat the mantra and worship Uchchhishta Matangini will have their desires satisfied and will gain control over foes.

According to the Pranotasani Tantra and Narad Pancharatna, Parvati expressed a desire to visit her maternal home for a few days and sought Shiva›s permission. Reluctantly, Shiva agreed but set a condition that if she did not return within a few days, he would come to bring her back. Parvati went to her father's place and stayed there for an extended period. Meanwhile, Shiva, longing for Parvati, disguised himself as an ornament seller and went to her. He sold her shell ornaments and, to test her fidelity, asked for sexual favours in return. Parvati, feeling disgusted, was about to curse the ornament seller with yogic powers realized that the ornament seller was none other than Shiva. She saw through his game and played along, agreeing to grant the favours, but at an appropriate time.

That evening, Parvati returned to Shiva's abode disguised as a Chandala (an outcaste) huntress and performed a seductive dance to entice him. She informed Shiva that she had come to engage in penance. Shiva responded by saying that he is the one who grants the fruits of all penances. He took her hand, kissed her, and they made love. During their intimate encounter, Shiva himself transformed into a Chandala and recognized the Chandala woman as his wife.

After their union, Parvati requested Shiva to grant her wish that her form as a Chandalini (the Chandala female form in which Shiva had made love to her) would endure forever as Uchchhishta Chandalini. She asked that her worship in this form precede Shiva's so that his worship would be considered fruitful.

The Dhyana mantra*s* in the Purashcharyarnava and the Tantrasara describe Matangi as a beautiful maiden with a blue complexion. She has a smiling face with three eyes and a little perspiration around the face, which adds to her charm and shiny complexion. She is resplendent with jewels from head to toe, with a crown that bears a crescent moon resting on her long hair. She sits on a bejewelled throne flanked by two parrots, playing a ruby-studded veena. In her four arms, she carries a noose, a mace, an axe, and a hook. In her manifestation as Ucchishtha Chandalini, she is depicted with a green complexion, seated on a corpse, holding a veena, a knife, a bowl of blood, and a skull on which is seated a parrot. She is surrounded by nature in the form of birds, especially parrots, which symbolically represent the presence of a guru.

Her blue or green complexion is related to her association with the planet Budha (Mercury), who is said to govern intelligence and wisdom. The parrot that she holds in her hand represents speech, and the veena symbolizes her association with music and the fine arts.

She governs the sense organ of the ear, which relates to the power of listening and the ability to understand speech. It is in the ear that the actual process of learning begins, as it is the means by which knowledge is received. The word Shruti means "that which is heard." The Vedas themselves are considered Shruti, indicating that they were not composed by humans but revealed by the divine through sound. The ear serves as the means to receive and transmit this sacred knowledge.

In Vedic times, the transmission of knowledge was primarily oral. Students would learn the Vedas directly from their gurus through listening and repetition. The ear played a crucial role in preserving the accuracy and integrity of the Vedic verses. The process of listening and reciting was considered sacred and was believed to ensure the purity of the teachings. The Vedas are chanted and recited with a specific emphasis on correct pronunciation and intonation. The rhythm, melody, and accentuation of the Vedic verses are believed to have a profound impact on the mind, body, and spirit.

The Vedas emphasize the importance of attentive listening as a means of acquiring knowledge and wisdom. The ear serves as the gateway through which divine vibrations and messages contained within these sacred verses are received.

Matangi represents the power of the spoken word (Vaikhari) when it turns into an embodiment of the thoughts conceived in the speaker's mind. She therefore has the ability to penetrate thought and the mind. Bhairavi represents Paravak, the transcendent and unmanifested speech; Tara stands for Pashyanti; and Matangi is associated, in addition to Vaikhari, with Madhyama, where ideas are formulated and translated into expression. This aspect of her role highlights her connection to the creative process of transforming thoughts and concepts into tangible communication. Therefore, while the spoken word is one aspect of her domain, she also governs other forms of inner thought and expression, including art, music, and dance.

Art, music, and dance are seen as powerful modes of expression and communication that transcend verbal language. Matangi's influence extends to these forms of creative expression, as they allow for the conveyance of emotions, ideas, and spiritual experiences beyond the limitations of spoken words. She is seen playing the veena, which is symbolic of her influence over music and the fine arts.

In her highest form, Matangi represents Para Vaikhari, which refers to the Supreme Word manifested through speech. This concept encompasses not only the spoken word but also the knowledge contained within the scriptures and sacred texts. Matangi is associated with deep wisdom, divine inspiration, and the ability to articulate and convey profound truths. By embracing and invoking the energy of Matangi, practitioners seek to enhance their abilities in speech, creativity, and communication. They aim to cultivate clarity, eloquence, and the capacity to express higher truths and inner knowledge through various artistic mediums.

As the embodiment of the Supreme Word and knowledge contained within the scriptures, She is called Mantrini, the mistress of the sacred mantras, having supremacy over all mantras, especially when they are uttered. She confers the ability to communicate with all the deities through the chanting of their specific mantras.

Matangi is described as dwelling in the Vishuddha, or throat chakra, the plexus of speech. She is also located at the level of the tip of the tongue, where speech is articulated. There is a subtle energy channel that runs from Ajna, the third eye chakra, to the tip of the tongue which is called Saraswati. This nadi, which facilitates the manifestation of divine inspiration through speech, is the energy manifestation of Matangi. Swami Yogi Ananda Saraswati writes: "The Saraswati Nadi is the stream of inspiration from the mind to its expression via speech. Matangi represents the flow of bliss through this channel, which is experienced by the creators of great literary, poetic, and other artistic works, resulting in brilliant expressions of creativity."

As the goddess of learning and speech, and the bestower of knowledge and talent, she also represents the word of a guru, who serves as a spiritual guide. A guru is one who offers the knowledge of the spiritual tradition that he embodies, to his disciples by means of the uttered word. A guru is also someone who represents the continuity of the spiritual tradition. He serves as a custodian of spiritual teachings, practices, and wisdom that have been passed down through generations and is responsible for transmitting this knowledge to students. In Hinduism, the guru-disciple relationship is based on a lineage, which represents an unbroken chain of spiritual transmission from ancient times to the present. The guru acts as a representative and bearer of this lineage, upholding its authenticity and preserving the integrity of the teachings. The guru initiates disciples into the spiritual tradition through specific rituals or ceremonies and then imparts knowledge. He serves as a living example, embodying the teachings and inspiring disciples through his presence, actions, and virtues.

According to David Frawley, Matangi's description as impure has a profound connection to the nature of the spoken word, which labels things and stereotypes them, thereby hindering actual contact with the soul of things. Matangi is described as one who helps a person go beyond the spoken word to seek the inner meaning and knowledge, that lie outside the demarcated boundaries of tradition. In this sense, she is the outcaste goddess, the Ucchisshta Chandalini present in any impurity.

The concept of impurity is not meant to be understood in a negative or derogatory sense, but rather as a symbol or representation of the inclusive nature of divinity and the spiritual path. In her manifestation as Uchchhishta Chandalini, she signifies her association with what is considered impure and unchaste. She is offered polluted, leftover food and is herself described as a leftover, symbolizing that it is pure divinity that is left over when all things eventually perish. It represents her ability to transcend conventional boundaries and accept offerings from all sources, regardless of their perceived purity or impurity.

Historically, outcastes or Chandalas were considered impure in the social hierarchy. Matangi's association with impurity is seen as an affirmation of her affinity for those who are rejected or excluded from mainstream society. It signifies her ability to embrace and uplift those who are marginalized or deemed impure, representing the divine acceptance and compassion that transcend social boundaries.

Matangi's connection with impurity can also be understood as a path of liberation through transgression. She is known as the goddess who breaks societal norms and challenges conventional boundaries. Matangi's association with impurity reflects her willingness to go beyond societal restrictions, dogmas, and limitations to attain spiritual freedom and self-realization. It signifies the potential for personal transformation by embracing and transcending societal judgments and limitations.

Our essential divine nature transcends all dualities of good and bad, pure and impure, clean and unclean. As long as we remain attached to these dualities, we cannot rise above the impurity of the manifested world. This is the lesson that we can learn from impurity, symbolically assigned to Matangi. She reveals to us the highest knowledge of this manifested world, which is considered impure when compared to the un-manifested world in its divine transcendence.

Matangi is closely connected with the energy of Ganesha, the revered and popular elephant-headed god, who is lord of the uttered word. In Sanskrit, Matangi means a female elephant and is symbolized by a strong and active elephant. Her thousand-name hymn from the Nanayavarta-tantra *describes* her as dwelling in, knowing, and relishing the forest, just as an elephant does. Since both Ganesha and Matangi are related to the elephant and learning, her energy can also be invoked to remove obstacles.

Meditation upon Matangi's esoteric aspects, such as her connection with the ear, with the guru, with nature, with the uttered word, and with Ganesha, provides a source of insight and inspiration into the mysterious workings of the divine in the Universe. In the Krishna Yajurveda, Mahanarayana Upanishad, Matangi is thus described:

"O goddess of intellect, favoured by you, one becomes a seer; one becomes a brahman, or a knower of the Supreme. Favoured by you, one becomes also possessed of riches. Favoured by you, one gains manifold wealth. Being such, O goddess of intellect, delight in us and confer on us wealth."

Kamalatmika – The Bestower of Abundance

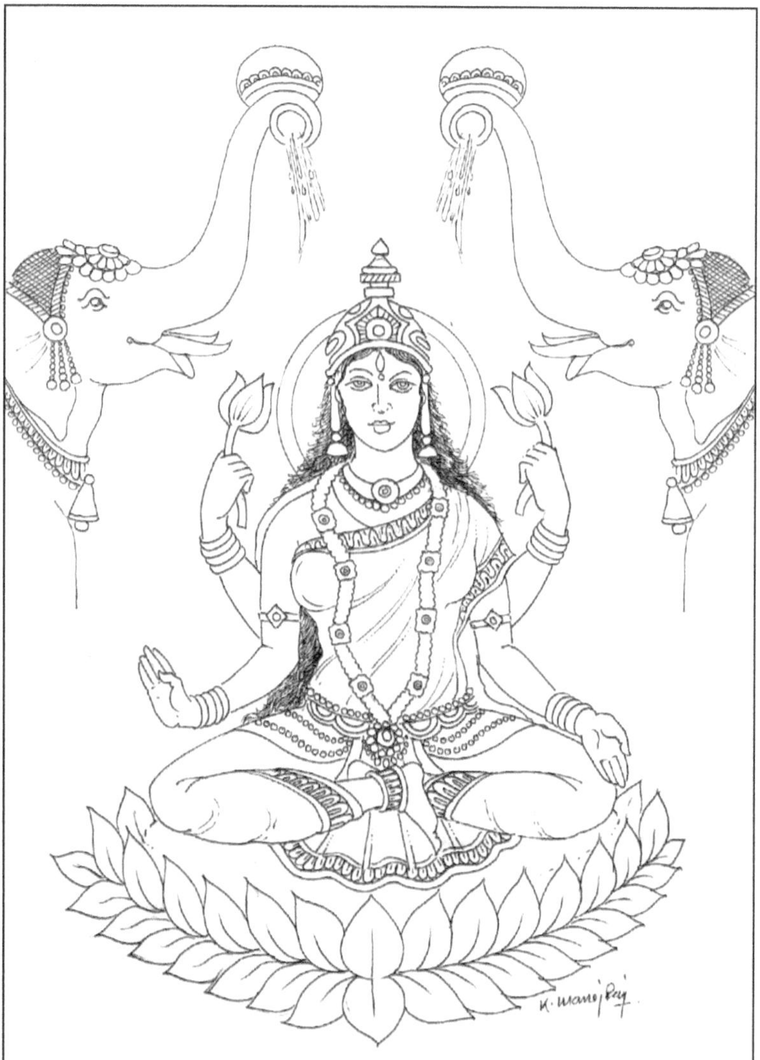

Kantya kanchana sannibham himagiri prakhyaish chaturbhir gajair
Hastoautkshipta hiranmaya amrita ghatair asichyamanam shriyam
Vibhranam varam abja yugmam abhayam hastaih kiritoaujvalam
Kshomabadha nitamba bimba lalitam vande aravinda sthitam

I meditate on Devi Kamalatmika

Whose splendour is like that of molten gold

Who is bathed with nectar from four golden pitchers

Lifted by the trunks and poured by four huge elephants

Whose appearances resemble the visible Himalayas

Who is Sri herself

She holds a pair of lotuses with her two hands and shows the gestures Of varada and abhaya with her other two hands

Her head is decorated with a shining diadem
Her lovely, rounded hips are bound by silken clothes
I worship that Devi who abides on a lotus

Tantra is a very precise science that leaves little place for coincidences, as each syllable, each dot, and each detail of a ritual are deliberate, well thought out, and accurately articulated. Hence, it is no surprise that we began the Mahavidya with Kali and ended them with the worship of Kamalatmika. Both names start with "ka", a syllable associated with the power of the Brahman, leading us to the realization that Kamalatmika is no less important because she is listed last. While Kali is all things fierce, Kamalatmika is all that is beautiful and abundant. While Kali represents the highest state of consciousness, Kamala is related to material wellbeing and worldly comforts. Kali is transcendental experience, while Kamalatmika is the reality of the 'here-and-now'.

Shakti created the universe, but she was dissatisfied as her task remained incomplete. The world needed prosperity and abundance to be wholesome and complete in all respects. To address this need, she manifested as Kamalatmika, whose purpose was to manifest wealth and prosperity in the world. When the appropriate time arrived, she was born as the daughter of Sage Bhrigu and brought abundance to the world. As a Tantric characterization of the goddess of prosperity, Lakshmi, she is the most benign of the Mahavidya goddesses, gentle, kind, and benevolent in all her aspects, representing the unfolding of inner consciousness into the fullness of creation.

Tantric texts describe Kamalatmika as emerging out of the Samudra Manthana, the churning of the milky ocean. Vedic texts point to a profound connection between water and the origins of life on Earth. Water is a fundamental element that plays a crucial role in the emergence and sustenance of life forms. Modern science and abiogenesis suggest that life on Earth originated in the primordial oceans. In the early stages of Earth's history, when the planet was rich in water and volcanic activity was prevalent, complex organic molecules formed in the oceans. These molecules eventually led to the development of self-replicating entities, marking the beginning of life. Water provides a nurturing environment for the development and evolution of life and forms an integral component of biological systems, serving as the primary constituent of cells and making up a significant portion of the human body and other organisms. Water is crucial for the continued existence of life on Earth, and the Vedic rishis and seers considered the vast oceans as creative consciousness itself.

Kamalatmika is described as having a beautiful, ever-smiling face with three lotus-shaped eyes. She has a golden complexion, resplendent like the rising sun, and wears a bright moon disc on her crown. She is adorned in beautiful silks, accessorized with sparkling jewels. She is being bathed by four large elephants, who pour jars of nectar over her. She holds lotuses in two of her hands, while the other two hands are in abhaya and varada mudra.

The most prominent motif in Kamaltmika is the recurrent lotus. She is shown seated in Padmasana, or lotus position. She wears a garland of lotuses and is surrounded by blossoming lotuses all around her. The lotus is regarded in Hinduism as a symbol of purity and spiritual enlightenment. The lotus rises from muddy waters to bloom above the surface representing the journey of the soul from ignorance to awakening. The unfolding petals of the lotus symbolize the gradual unravelling of one's spiritual potential.

The lotus is associated with divine birth and creation, as several deities and divine beings are depicted as emerging from a lotus. Brahma, the creator of the universe, is seen sitting on a lotus that emerges from the navel of Lord Vishnu. The lotus represents the ability to transcend worldly limitations and attain spiritual perfection. Just as the lotus blooms above the water, untouched by the impurities below, it symbolizes rising above material desires and attachments. It also symbolizes spiritual growth and transformation, signifying the journey of the soul from its roots in earthly existence to the blossoming of higher consciousness. The lotus roots in the mud represent the human attachment to worldly experiences, while the blossoming flower represents the realization of divinity and the attainment of spiritual liberation. Kamalatmika is the spiritual lotus on which universal energy is based and blooms in the void, coming forth in the space of pure consciousness.

The second most prominent motif associated with Kamalatmika is the elephant. Four elephants, representing fertility and sovereignty, surround her and bathe her in copious amounts of nectar, according to Tantric texts. They are as white as the Himalayan snow. In Hinduism, the elephant is considered a sacred and revered animal, regarded as a symbol of wisdom, intelligence, and knowledge. Its large size and perceived intelligence have made it a representation of wisdom and intellectual capabilities. The elephant is admired for its strength, power, and might. Its ability to overcome obstacles and its sheer physical presence make it a symbol of strength and endurance. In iconography, the elephant is depicted as a vahana (vehicle) for various deities, including Lord Indra, the king of gods, who rides on an elephant named Airavata.

The elephant is associated with prosperity, abundance, and good fortune. In Hindu culture, it is believed that the presence of an elephant on auspicious occasions and festivals brings blessings and positive energy. The showering of water by elephants during religious ceremonies is seen as a symbol of purification and prosperity.

Elephants are known for their loyalty, obedience, and strong familial bonds. They are seen as a bridge between the earthly and divine realms. Their massive presence and grounding nature symbolize their connection to the material world, while their association with deities and elevated status in mythology connect them to the spiritual realm.

Kamalatmika shares many important attributes with Lakshmi. They are both givers of prosperity, fertility, and good luck. Both are referred to as Sri, which stands for all that is auspicious and radiant. Sri is a sacred prefix or honorific used before the names of deities, indicating their supreme and auspicious nature, closely associated with good fortune and blessings. It is believed that invoking the name or presence of Sri brings positive energy, prosperity, and divine grace. The term is used in prayers, hymns, and rituals to seek blessings and invoke divine favour.

The visual representation of Sri in the form of a mystical symbol is considered highly auspicious and is used in religious rituals, adornments, and sacred objects. Sri also carries the symbolism of spiritual transformation and elevation. It represents the divine path towards liberation, enlightenment, and self-realization. The Sri Suktam, a hymn from the Rigveda, is a composition dedicated to Sri, consisting of sixteen verses that extol her qualities. It describes her as the radiant goddess who bestows wealth, prosperity, and happiness upon her devotees, highlighting her benevolence, grace, beauty, and abundance.

The Sri Suktam emphasizes the significance of invoking and honouring Sri for material and spiritual well-being. It is recited during special occasions and festivals (such as Diwali and Lakshmi Puja), accompanied by other Vedic chants and rituals. It is considered a powerful invocation and expression of gratitude towards the goddess, seeking her blessings and grace in both the material and spiritual realms. The Satapatha Brahmana, another important Vedic composition, relates Kamaltmika to abundance of food, the power and lustre of royalty, good fortune, and beauty.

The lotus is used as a symbol to represent and visualize the seven chakras. Chakras can be described as spinning wheels or vortexes of energy that regulate and distribute prana throughout the body. They are an integral part of the subtle body system and play a crucial role in physical, mental, and spiritual well-being.

Kamalatmika, as the Lotus Goddess, governs the chakras in the human body. The lotus symbolizes the blooming and opening of consciousness as it grows from the muddy waters and rises above to bloom. In the same way, the chakras unfold and develop as one progresses on the spiritual path. Each chakra is depicted as having a number of petals, representing the different qualities, energies, and aspects associated with that chakra.

In meditation and visualization practices, the lotus is seen as blossoming at each chakra, symbolizing the activation and harmonization of that particular energy centre. This visualization can facilitate the flow of prana through the chakras, leading to their balance and healing.

Kamalatmika has the ability to create beauty and prosperity even when bleakness persists. Her bija mantra is "eem", a primal Shakti seed mantra from which the other important bijas such as Hreem, Kleem, and Shreem are derived. "Eem" is therefore known as the yoni bija, that which gives birth to the other bijas.

At its core, beauty carries an element of the transcendent. When we encounter true beauty, whether it be in nature, art, music, or even human connections, it transcends the ordinary and touches something deep within us. It awakens our senses, stirs our emotions, and resonates with our innermost being. It has the power to inspire awe, wonder, and a sense of reverence. In those moments, we often feel a deep connection to something greater than ourselves, something that transcends the physical world and taps into a spiritual dimension.

The experience of true beauty can be a gateway to a heightened state of awareness, where we become more attuned to the mysteries and wonders of existence. It can awaken a sense of interconnectedness, reminding us that we are part of a larger tapestry of life. We feel a sense of unity with the world around us, recognizing that the same essence that imbues beauty in one thing exists in everything else as well.

In this spiritual encounter with true beauty, we experience a sense of transcendence beyond our individual selves. It can provide a glimpse into a deeper reality, inviting us to contemplate the nature of existence, the mysteries of the universe, and our place within it. It can evoke feelings of gratitude, reverence, and a longing for something beyond the mundane.

Moreover, the experience of true beauty can be transformative. It can inspire us to live more authentically, to seek harmony and balance in our lives, and to cultivate qualities such as compassion, love, and creativity. It can serve as a reminder of the inherent goodness and potential within ourselves and others.

An encounter with true beauty is a deeply personal and subjective experience. It can touch the core of our being, resonating with our spiritual nature and opening us up to a deeper understanding of ourselves and the world around us. It invites us to embark on a journey of exploration and discovery, where we continually seek and appreciate the beauty that exists in all facets of life, leading us closer to our spiritual essence.

David Frawley, in his book Tantric Yoga and the Wisdom Goddesses writes: "Kamala is Lakshmi among the Dasa Mahavidya. Lakshmi is the Goddess of wealth, beauty, fertility, love, and devotion, like Roman Venus and Greek Aphrodite, who, like Lakshmi, are born from the ocean, but on a sea shell rather than a lotus. Lakshmi is the great Mother in her role of fulfilling all desires. She represents the water of fulfilment, the flowering of Divine grace and love. Kamala is similar to Tripura Sundari in that both rule over love, beauty, and bliss. Tripura Sundari, however, rules over the subtle form of bliss born of perception of the Self. Kamala governs the outer form of beauty, not merely as pleasure but as the unfolding of the Divine nature into the realms of action and creation."

Kamala supports our worldly activities and aspirations by promoting the fulfilment of our pursuit of pleasure, wealth, and fame. She reveals to us, slowly, like the unfolding of the lotus petals, the various layers of existence and compels us to seek divine fulfilment even as we pursue Dharma—righteousness, duty, and moral obligations; Artha—material well-being, wealth, and prosperity; Kama—pleasure, desire, and sensual enjoyment—and ultimately the goal of human life, Moksha or liberation. Kamalatmika's lesson for us lies in showing us how the four Purusharthas are interconnected and are meant to be pursued in a balanced and harmonious manner.

Kamalatmika is one of the most worshipped goddesses in the Hindu pantheon. Her imagery is the basis of Hindu calendar art, with every home and office incomplete without a picture of her beaming down upon her devotees with her radiant smile and ever-giving hands. Every human being seeks the presence of this goddess, who is the embodiment of prosperity, wealth, and happiness. Invoking her and acquiring her blessings assures us an abundance of all things we value in life: food (as she is linked to the fertility of soil and harvesting of crops), fertility, happiness, beauty, good fortune, and material wealth. She gives us an opportunity to experience the pleasures of this beautiful world.

Our Vedic texts emphasize the idea that we as humans are entitled to experience enjoyment and pleasure in our lives, recognizing our natural inclinations and desires to fulfil these wishes, which bring temporary happiness and contentment. Bhoga, especially in Tantra philosophy, is not always seen to be in contrast to the ultimate goal of Moksha. Tantra suggests ways to strike a balance between Bhoga and the pursuit of Moksha. It recognizes that excessive attachment and indulgence in worldly pleasures can lead to suffering and perpetuate the cycle of desire and dissatisfaction. Therefore, while Bhoga is considered a legitimate aspect of human life, Tantra advises to pursue it in moderation and within the framework of Dharma to avoid negative consequences and to maintain a harmonious existence.

As the tenth of the Great Goddesses in the Mahavidya tradition, Kamalatmika completes the sequence of the guiding wisdom of the sacred feminine. She is placed last as the culmination of final wisdom, to be, as David Frawley suggests "the full unfoldment of the power of the Goddess into the material sphere". She is intentionally placed last in order to create a sense of anticipation and then finally reveal a deep bond between the creator and creation. This bond is portrayed as a form of alchemy, involving the creation, concealment, and eventual revelation of beauty within all aspects of creation.

Kamalatmika encourages us to look beyond the surface and seek a deeper understanding that connects everything and resonates with a sense of unity. By peering beneath the superficial aspects and delving into the essence of things, we can discover the universal beauty and interconnectedness that bind all of creation together and the fundamental essence that exists within all of creation.

Mantras and Yantras of Dasa Mahavidya

Usually, the worship of Mahavidya energies is undertaken by Tantra practitioners who have dedicated their lives to seeking the divine. For the common man, the two simplest ways to approach the powerful energies of these Shakti goddesses are through the use of mantra and yantra. It is said in the Sri Mahakala Samhita, Guhyakali Khanda, that no puja of Kali is complete without the worship of her mantra and yantra. These energies can be accessed at various levels, ranging from performing a simple puja as part of the daily ritual and incorporating the yantra as a tool for meditation while chanting the mantra to engaging in elaborate rituals such as havan and yagna, which involve temporary drawing of the yantra and doing japa of the mantra.

Mantras

Mananaat traayate iti mantrah

That which uplifts us by continuous repetition is a 'mantra'

Chanting is an ancient practice that has played an integral role in all religious and spiritual traditions across the globe since time immemorial. The repeated recitation of a divine name is common to Hinduism, Islam, Christianity, Buddhism, Judaism, and even pagan and shamanic traditions. Chanting is best described as the rhythmic repetition (either silently or aloud) of a sound, word, prayer, or song. It is an established fact that sound has tremendous power.

The Sanskrit word for sound is Nada. In Hindu tradition, it is believed that the entire universe is made up of sound vibrations called Nada. Nada is of two types: Ahata and Anahata. Ahata is a sound produced through contact (clapping of hands, hitting a drum, etc.), vibration (from striking the chord of a sitar or veena), and obstruction (blowing into a flute or a trumpet). Anahata is the sound that exists in the universe as a cosmic hiss that is eternal and cannot be produced. A sound, therefore, is a pulsation or vibration—a form of energy that exists throughout the universe and can be harnessed to help align ourselves better with the higher forces of nature.

The purpose of chanting is to bring about silence in the ever-chattering mind. The process of repetition of a word or set of words helps bring about a temporary state of mindfulness as the brain is completely absorbed in the activity of repetition. Chanting is a very useful step in the process of meditation, as it offers a vehicle for the mind to transport itself to a higher realm.

The Kamakoti Mandali, which comprises a close-knit group of Sri Vidya practitioners, describes how mantras work: "A human being is composed of various layers or types of bodies, and the Parashakti pervades and illuminates all these bodies through different aspects of prana assimilated through mechanisms such as breathing for the Sthula Sharira, etc., The energetic link between the lower and higher bodies is the breath, or prana, and the path to transcendence lies in its neutralization. Every technique of upasana is, in one way or another, aimed at modifying the breath or prana so as to refine it and intensify awareness of the subtle and inner breath-current connected with the higher bodies. The simplest way to accomplish this is through the might of unmoving attention directed towards an external or internal object, with breath itself being an important option. The acts of silencing the mind and the breath are interconnected, and mantra is an important way to accomplish both. The generally chaotic mind is regulated through powerful waves of energy generated by the mantra, and the focused attention of the sadhaka on the mantra acts as a means to sublimate the breath and the mind."

The Sanskrit word mantra can be broken up into man meaning mind and tra meaning tool or instrument. The vibrations created by the sound and the focus on rhythmic pronunciation have a profound effect on the body and mind. The nervous system experiences a slowdown of activities and a calmness that descends reduces stress, high blood pressure, and pain and improves immunity.

Dr. David Frawley, a renowned Ayurveda expert, says that "a mantra, when carefully chosen and used silently, has the ability to help alter your subconscious impulses, habits, and afflictions. Mantras, when spoken or chanted, direct the healing power of prana (life force energy) and, in traditional Vedic practices, can be used to energize and access spiritual states of consciousness."

Each of the Dasa Mahavidya is associated with several mantras, ranging from a single bija to thousand-word eulogies chanted in their praise. The mantras I have listed here are the simple bija mantras, which can invoke the blessings and power of a specific energy and can be chanted without initiation from a guru.

Here are the mantras associated with each of the Dasa Mahavidya:

1. Kali: "Om Kreem Kalikaye Namah"

2. Tara: "Om Hreem Streem Hum Phat"

3. Tripura Sundari: "Om Aim Hreem Shreem Tripura Sundariye Namah"

4. Bhuvaneshwari: "Om Hreem Bhuvaneshwaryai Namah"

5. Bhairavi: "Hreem Hreem Bhairavi Bhairavi Hreem Hreem"

6. Chinnamasta: "Om Shreem Hreem Shreem Chandramukhiyei Namah"

7. Dhumavati: "Om Dhum Dhumavatyai Namah"

8. Bagalamukhi: "Om Hreem Bagalamukhi Sarvadushtanam Vacham Mukham Padam Stambhaya Jivham Keelaya Buddhim Vinashaya Hreem Om Swaha"

9. Matangi: "Om Hreem Matangyai Namah"

10. Kamala: "Om Hreem Shreem Kleem Kamalvaasinyai Namah"

These are a few steps to keep in mind as you begin chanting:

- Sit up straight with your spine erect.

- Gently close the eyes and focus on your breath for a few minutes as the body begins to relax.

- Choose the mantra of the goddess whose energy resonates with your life situation at the given point in time. If you wish to achieve financial stability, then chant the Lalita Tripura Sundari mantra while meditating on the Sri Yantra. If you seek better health, chant the Bhuvaneshwari mantra. If you wish to overcome obstacles, chant the Dhumavati mantra. Use your intuitive awareness to determine which mantra and yantra appeal to you the most. This can vary from day to day and season to season, and that is natural and acceptable.

- At first, repeat the mantra aloud, focusing on pronunciation and duration. Make sure you chant the words at the same pace. Keep track of the number of breaths between the words to help keep pace.

- Listen to the mantra and repeat it, allowing the words to permeate your whole being.

- Feel the vibrations as they occur within the body, and be mindful of all the sensations.

- With practice, you will feel that your voice is getting deeper and gathering more power. Use this as motivation to further your spiritual growth.

- Practice chanting every day for 10 to 15 minutes to begin with, and then increase it to 30 minutes as the practice improves.

- You can practice with a Japa mala (similar to a rosary but with 108 beads) to help maintain the count.

Yantras

Swami Shantananda Puri Maharaj says: "In order to bring a vast object like the river Ganga from a place far away, one has to use a limited vessel. Similarly, in order to bring the eternal essence of cosmic energy and beyond, Upasakas use Yantras."

All spiritual traditions have upheld the belief that everything in the cosmos is energy (it is called chi, qi, prana, etc., in different cultures) and that every aspect of existence is deeply interwoven in this giant web of energy. Modern advances in science, especially studies in Quantum Mechanics, have led to a vindication of this long-held belief that "everything is energy," as scientists realized that all particles are merely vibrations of energy. If the universe is pure energy and we are but a small part of this same energy, then it stands to reason that there is a possibility for us, as individuals, to tune into the frequency of the universe's energy.

There are several methods of tuning in such as through the power of sound, crystals, meditation, or prayer. One such powerful method is by using symbols as a tuning fork. Just as we are able to tune into a specific channel on television or on the radio by selecting a particular frequency, these symbols give us the ability to tune in and engage with the powers of creation in the Universe. A yantra is a graphic and geometric representation of the Universal energy, which acts like a tuning fork.

Thoughts and words cannot exist in the spiritual dimension since they are constructs of the intellect and mind. Sacred geometry arises from the fact that many philosophical truths cannot be expressed in words. The world around us is filled with geometrical designs and shapes. Ancient cultures, including those of the Greeks, Egyptians, Chinese, Mayans, and Hindus, observed that certain geometric patterns are found recurring throughout nature (spirals, hexagons, and concentric circles, to name a few) and believed them to be the building blocks of all creation in the universe.

The word yantra is derived from the root verb yantr, meaning to restrain or control. It can be understood as a machine or a device that controls human effort in performing a task by providing assistance. A mantra uses sound energy to bring about a balance between the mind and the body, while a yantra uses the visual medium to bring about a state of equilibrium.

A yantra can work as a transformer of our psychic energies, allowing us a glimpse into the beauty and power of the universe. There are hundreds of yantra designs that are specific to planets, gods, and principles. These geometric patterns can be drawn out on the floor in the form of rangoli (kollam), painted on paper or tree bark, or etched on metal sheets such as copper, silver, or gold.

Hinduism is full of ancient and sacred geometric symbols: Om, swastika, linga, and vaastu purusha, to name a few. They all hold the key to unraveling the secrets of the cosmos. We come across three terms that are commonly used in Hindu symbolism: Mandala, Chakra, and Yantra.

The term mandala appears in the Rig Veda and is used generically to stand for any drawing, diagram, or geometric pattern that represents the cosmos symbolically or metaphysically.

One of the chief purposes of the mandala is to represent the different layers of the universe—the spiritual realm, the environment we live in, and the inner experience of man—and how each of these layers can flow into and out of the next. Therefore, the mandala is perhaps the most essential tool for practitioners seeking to make a spiritual connection.

The Sanskrit word "chakra" essentially denotes a spinning vortex or wheel. In The Tantra of Sri Chakra Bhavanopanishat by Prof. S.K. Ramachandra Rao, he writes:

The etymology of the word would suggest that by which anything is done (kriyate aneana). The wheel of the cart, the wheel of the potter, and the wheel-like weapon that is flung against the enemy are all called 'chakras.' In its extended meaning, chakra also signifies a kingdom because the wheels of the king's chariot can roll in there without hindrance. The king of the land is thus described as chakra-vartin.

The most common form of mandala is the powerful, mystical, esoteric, and compelling yantra. It is said that Lord Shiva created 64 yantras and gave them to mankind to help them progress materially and spiritually. A yantra is considered to be the residence of its Ishta Devata and therefore, yantras are named after specific desires and gods and goddesses and are a representation of the energies they signify and embody.

Juan Carlos Ramchandani explains, "Each yantra is a mantra (sacred phoneme) by means of which the individual mind calls upon the cosmic energy through the three bodies: causal, subtle, and material. In addition, the yantras are complemented with mantras, since they combine the power of the practitioner with that of the yantra, which, in turn, vibrates with the infinite power of the universe. In meditation, both instruments are used simultaneously. A properly energized yantra contains the same energy of divinity and is the essence of divinity."

Every yantra has to conform to three basic principles:

- Akriti-rupa or Form

- Kriya-rupa or Function

- Shakti-rupa or Power

Through constant ritualistic worship, a yantra sheds its dormancy and becomes emblematic of spiritual power. The yantra, therefore, moves from mere form and function to become a power diagram.

Yantras are classified according to their uses, as below:

Type of Yantra	Its uses
Sharira Yantra	Yantras for the body, such as the chakras
Dharana Yantra	Those worn on the body to offer protection, ward off disease, etc., such as medallions and talismans
Asan Yantra	Those placed under the seat of a deity or meditation mat, or under the ground before the construction of a building, temple, etc.
Mandala Yantra	A live yantra is formed by nine persons, with eight sitting in eight cardinal directions and one in the centre to perform the puja or worship
Puja Yantra	Yantras, installed in temples, homes, or offices, to which regular worship is offered
Chattar Yantra	Those kept under a turban, hat, cap, or in the pocket
Darshan Yantra	Yantras believed to bring good fortune upon its viewer, are placed in temple, home or office

The geometric symmetry that lies within a yantra is a reflection of the unity of the individual with the universe, and the pattern of repetition of seeing the microcosm in the macrocosm and vice versa is said to bring about a balance in the two hemispheres of the brain.

Recent studies have shown that merely looking at certain geometric patterns can alter brain waves and open gateways to higher states of consciousness. The reason why this can happen is that the geometric patterns bring about an alignment of the left and right aspects of the brain. The left hemisphere of the brain is involved in verbal, analytical, and logic-related activities, while the right side performs more intuitive, creative, and holistic thinking tasks. Visualizing or meditating upon a yantra has been shown to bring about greater balance in the left and right sides of the brain.

One of the most powerful, auspicious, and important yantras in the Tantra tradition is the Sri Chakra Yantra. Tantric texts state that worship of any deity can be undertaken in the Sri Chakra, as it is the foundation of all yantras.

Swami Ayyappa Giri, Purohit-Acharya, Yogini Ashram, California, says: "A yantra is not limited as a divine manifestation. A Yantra literally holds the energy of a particular deity. A yantra is verily a geometric pattern that contains both an energy and a deity's spirit and is also a representation of a sound vibration (mantra). In worshiping the presiding deity of a yantra, we are acknowledging their presence both microcosmically, as the soul within ourselves (Jiva), and macrocosmically, as universal nature (Prakriti). Tantra teaches that from Purusha, the primal cause of the creation impulse, emerged Prakriti, or mother nature. The yantra is understood to be a mirror of the inner universal soul (Jiva). Its internal reflection of cosmic principles is inferred by the Tantric. In this way, the yantra, acting as a carrier of its representative energy, is massively empowering."

The following are the yantras associated with each of the Mahavidya:

Kali

Om Kreem Kalikaye Namah

Tara

Om Hreem Streem Hum Phat

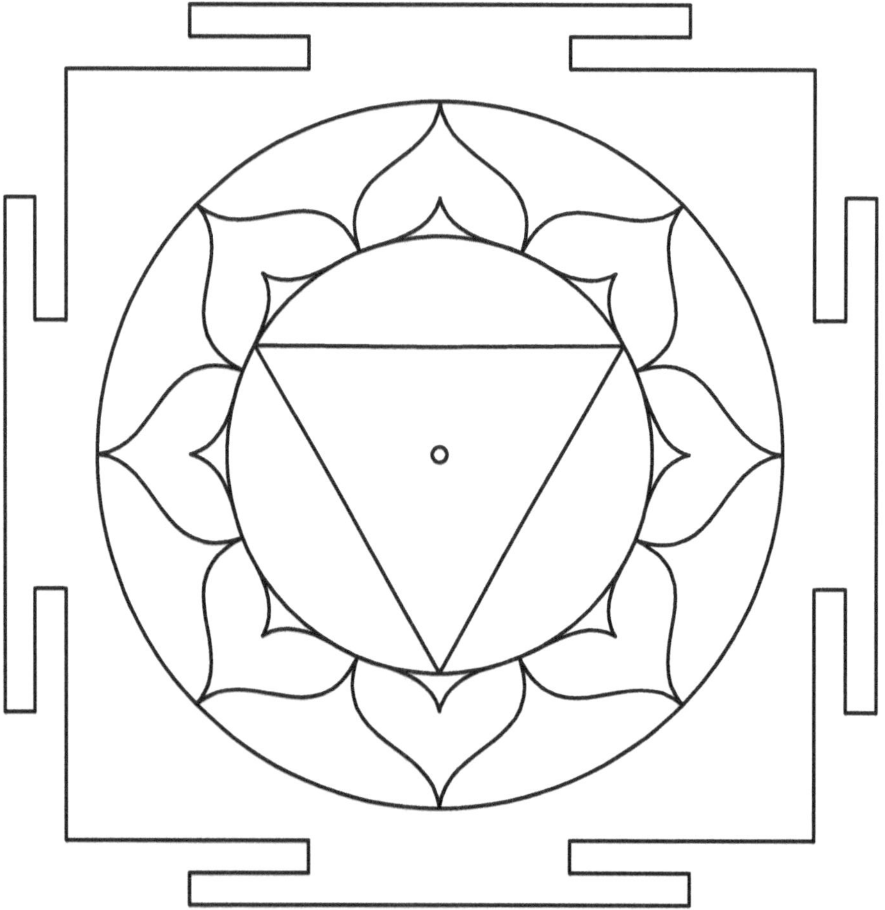

Lalita Tripura Sundari

Om Aim Hreem Shreem Tripura Sundariye Namah

Bhuvaneshwari

Om Hreem Bhuvaneshwaryai Namah

Bhairavi

Hreem Hreem Bhairavi Bhairavi Hreem Hreem

Chhinamasta

Om Shreem Hreem Shreem Chandramukhiyei Namah

Dhumavati

Om Dhum Dhumavatyai Namah

Bagalamukhi

Om Hreem Bagalamukhi Sarvadushtanam Vacham Mukham
Padam Stambhaya Jivham Keelaya Buddhim Vinashaya Hreem
Om Swaha

Matangi

Om Hreem Matangyai Namah

Kamalatmika

Om Hreem Shreem Kleem Kamalvaasinyai Namah

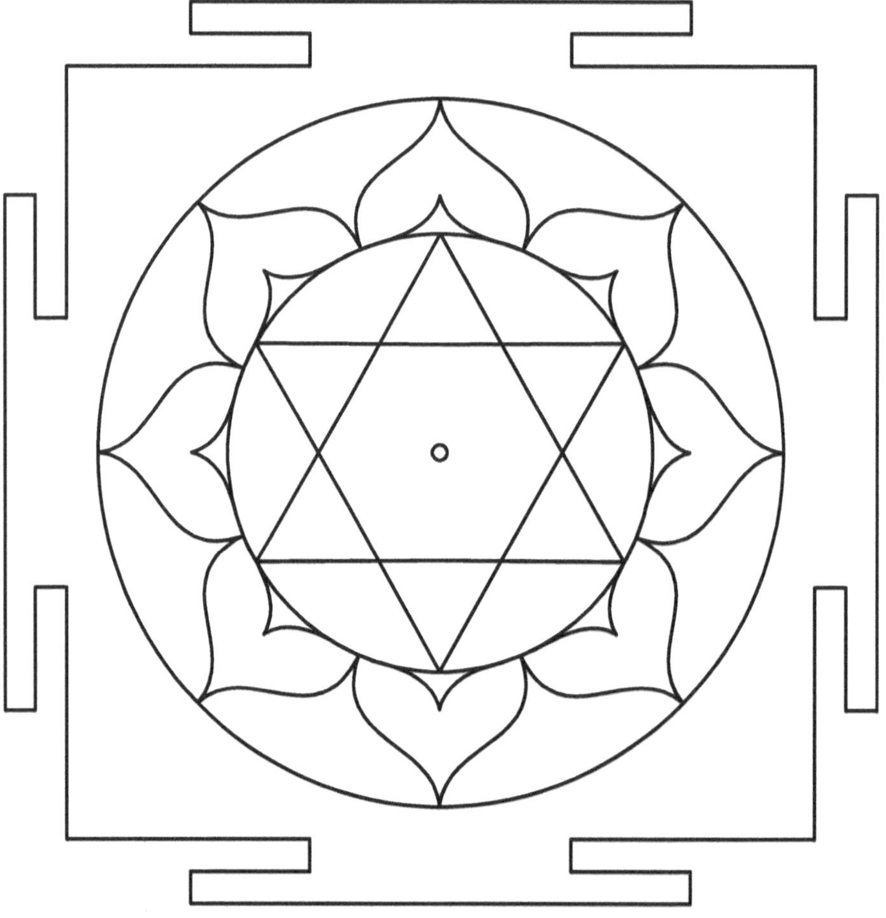

Here are some recommendations for Yantra worship:

1. Take a black-and-white printout of the yantra associated with the energy that resonates most with you at any given point in time.

2. Place the drawing in the East or North-East direction, facing the West, at eye level.

3. There are two ways of meditating on any yantra. You can start on the outer periphery and move inwards towards the Bindu, or centre point, or begin with the Bindu and slowly extend your vision towards the boundaries of the yantra. Both are acceptable, and you can choose whichever appeals to you instinctively.

4. Once you feel comfortable with a certain yantra, you should buy a copper plate engraved with accurate geometry, as it is more potent and can be permanently installed.

5. You can also draw the yantra on paper using a pen or pencil, as this serves as an excellent way to connect with the energies embedded within the sacred geometry.

6. While meditating on the yantra or while drawing, chant the specific mantra associated with the energy for a heightened result.

7. Make a Sankalpa or state your intention if you wish to achieve a specific outcome before your meditation, as thoughts and desires get amplified through the yantra.

It is ideal to practice mantra and yantra sadhana on a regular basis, possibly once a week or twice a month on full moon days (poornavasya) and new moon days (amavasya), on special days such as birthdays, anniversaries, etc., and during the four Navratris that are celebrated in the year as per the Hindu calendar.

Conclusion

Devaan bhavaya tanena
Te devah bhavayantu vah
Parasparam bhavayanta Shreya
Param vapsyatah

Chapter 3, verse 11 of the Bhagavat Gita describes that the purpose of creating a divine entity is to reflect the action back on the devotee, thereby raising his vibration as ascribed by the deity. The devotee breathes life into the deity each time he meditates upon his Ishta Devata. With this, we nourish the gods, and may the gods nourish us, thus nourishing one another to attain the highest good.

Undoubtedly, the Mahavidya, as a group of individual deities, depict some of the most unusual, fierce, strange, and vivid gods ever portrayed in any major world religion or culture. The forms are radically different from the benign and beautiful gods worshipped in cultured society. They challenge accepted norms of social order with their outlandish behaviour, grotesque bodies, ugly faces, and bizarre habits. These outrageous manifestations are meant to shock us and compel us to look beyond our comfort zones. The disturbing and distressing aspects force us to look deeper into ourselves to identify our shortcomings and show us for what we are, not what we are meant to be. By rejecting and subverting conventionally accepted norms, the Mahavidya seeks to expand awareness and liberate the mind from inhibitions and prejudices.

In Tantra, Satchidananda (the eternal, unchanging nature of reality), where Sat stands for existence, Chit denotes awareness, and Ananda embodies bliss. Man is identical to this ultimate reality, but he forgets his true nature as he comes under the influence of Maya, or illusion. He takes this apparent world of subject and object to be real and therefore undergoes suffering and bondage. The goal of Tantra is to cultivate a spiritual discipline that will lead to the rediscovery of man's true identity, which is the same as the ultimate reality.

Every human wants to enjoy the material pleasures of this world, and he is entitled to experience the beauty of creation. Once the desire is fulfilled, it no longer remains a point of obsession or interest. It is this aspect of human nature that Tantra fully understands and therefore allows, if not actually encourages, the seeker to fulfil all desires, however taboo they may appear to society.

Manblunder writes in his blog on Tantra: "For tantric practitioners, nothing is right and nothing is wrong, as everything is Shiva. Everything in its sadhana is aimed at satisfying the senses and comes from a profound understanding of human nature. Tantric novices do not leave a single hidden residue, a single unsatisfied desire, or a single dream remaining within. Any experience linked to ego, desire, or possession has nothing to do with Tantrism. When Shiva penetrates Shakti, it is a complete sacred act. All repressions that are not flushed out or satisfied, produce bouts of thought processes and evade the realization of Shiva. They will never achieve divine spontaneity."

It is natural to wonder about the reason why our ancient seers divided all the great knowledge into ten diverse aspects. Vedic scholars have indicated that it was an effort to drive home specific essential points:

1. The Divine Mother is absolute, ineffable, immutable, and beyond time and space.

2. In the act of creation, she subjects herself to the constraints of time and space. Time is an aspect of Prakruti (Nature) and one of the thirty six tattvas, or principles of creation. However, as a concept, it is a creation of our intellect based on our sensory perception. It is a part of Maya or the illusory state in which we all exist. For the Divine Consciousness, there is no division of time; there is only the present moment, a continuous and undivided state of existence.

Space is vast and beyond our comprehension. It is infinite, without a beginning or an end. To simplify matters, we divide it into ten Disha, or the ten cardinal directions: East, West, North, South, South-East, South-West, North-east, North-West, above, and below. Disha implies not only direction but also dimension. There are ten dimensions of manifested creation represented by the ten Mahavidya energies, each with its own consciousness, awareness, and intelligence.

Even though each of these energies describes different knowledge and truths, ultimately all knowledge is one but is understood in ten different ways based on our five sense organs and five organs of action – skin, eye, ear, nose, tongue, mouth, foot, hand, anus, and genitalia. In the same way, truth is one, but we perceive it in various facets, shapes, forms, and meanings.

Shankaranarayanan says in his article on The Ten Great Cosmic Powers: "Each has a particular cosmic function and leads to a special realization of the One Reality. The might of Kali, the sound force of Tara, the beauty and bliss of Sundari, the vast vision of Bhuvaneshwari, the effulgent charm of Bhairavi, the striking force of Chhinnamasta, the silent inertness of Dhumavati, the paralyzing power of Bagalamukhi, the expressive play of Matangi, and the concord and harmony of Kamala is the various characteristics, the distinct manifestations of the Supreme

Consciousness, that have made this creation possible. The Tantra says that the Supreme can be realized at these various points."

Each one of the Mahavidya holds particular significance as a Brahmavidya. Together as a group, they contain all the wisdom of the universe—of the past, present, and future—and all the potential that has ever existed or will exist. A dedicated learner who seeks with devotion will be guided and inspired to find the spiritual strength and capability lying dormant within him to have his dreams manifested through a study of these great systems of knowledge. Bhairavi, Bhuvaneshwari, and Chinnamasta are called Vidya; Dhumavathi, Bagalamukhi, Matangi, and Kamala are called Siddhi Vidya; and the forms of Kali and Tara are considered to be Mahavidya. Tripurasundari is called Sri Vidya.

Dasa Mahavidya derives much of its importance from its association with Sri Vidya, the most popular and esoteric practice of the Tantra tradition, which is practiced by millions across the world. Vidya is the sacred knowledge of the ritual worship of Lalita Tripura Sundari using mantras such as the Panchadashi and Shodashi, along with meditation on her yantra (the Sri Chakra Yantra), all of which come together to form Sri Vidya.

Vidya means knowledge (vid means to know), learning, discipline, and a system of thought, and when the word Sri is prefixed to it, it becomes knowledge which is auspicious, beneficial, and conducive to prosperity. Sri is also the name given to the Mother Goddess who rules over the universe (tvam sris tvam isvari). She is called the mother because all living beings depend on her for the fulfilment of their destiny.

Swami Veda Bharati writes in an article titled What is Sri Vidya?: "Sri was a title originally reserved in ancient times for those who were initiated into Sri Vidya—those in whom God's glory of the universe has made a home, those who are endowed with knowledge, empowered with the energy and intuition of Mother Sri. The basic text of Sri Vidya says: One who knows Mother Sri can never be orphaned. In the rituals and ceremonies of the Indian tradition, when one sips the holy water, they say, Mayi Shrih Shrayatam: may Sri dwell in me. The word for refuge is Ashraya, meaning to be one as Sri. May many come taking refuge in me; may I seek refuge in none is the prayer of those who wish to have this capacity to give refuge. This capacity is Sri. One might translate Sri Vidya as the science of capacities, the science of potentialities."

In the Kubjika Tantram, Lord Shiva defines Sri Vidya as:

Sridatri cha sada vidya srividya parikirtita

The vidya that renders prosperity and abundance is called
Sri Vidya.

Our ancient texts and modern gurus are all in agreement on one aspect of Sri Vidya: in order for a person to practice this elegant and powerful discipline, one must have done thousands of years of sadhana in previous lives. It is said:

Athava paschimam janma athava shankarah swayam

This knowledge only becomes available to one who is in his or her final birth or is truly Shiva Himself. Our seers point out that if a person who is not deserving of initiation into the practice is still lucky enough to be exposed to this valuable knowledge based on some good karmas from the past, such a person may not reach self-realization in this lifetime but will surely enjoy a head start in his next life.

Sri Vidya is not a philosophy like Advaita Vedanta or Sankhya; at best, it can be termed an Upasana paddhati or a practice-related science. Most of the Sri Vidya texts are focused more on the practical aspects of how to acquire this knowledge than on its philosophy. Swami Amritananda Natha Saraswati says Sri Vidya is Advaita in action precisely because it stands at a point where soaring philosophical theory transforms into experience and outcomes.

Sri Vidya practice comprises Tantra, whose two main elements are Mantra and Yantra. A simple analogy would be to think of the Yantra as a car, the Mantra as its fuel, and the Tantra as the driving skill of the Sadhaka. The driver uses his mental faculties to navigate the car purposefully. In the same way, the Sadhaka uses Yantra and Mantra to reach his goal of connecting with the universal consciousness.

There are two approaches to understanding Sri Vidya:

1. Srishti krama (the basis of creation)

2. Samhara krama (the basis of dissolution)

Srishti karma is the process of delving into the secrets behind the process of creation. Lalita Tripura Sundari is worshipped first, and from her all the other goddesses are extracted until all are in their rightful places. This is translated into a meditation of the Sri Chakra Yantra starting from the Bindu, which is the seat of the goddess, to its outer boundaries, traversing through the nine avaranas.

The word Samhara means absorption and merger. Each of the goddesses is worshiped and is absorbed into the next until we reach Lalita Tripura Sundari, in whom all the goddesses are absorbed. In Sri Chakra Yantra meditation, we begin at the outer boundaries of the yantra and move inward through the nine avaranas to eventually reach the Bindu and be one with the goddess.

These two approaches are balanced when one studies Sri Vidya and the practitioner uses Srishti krama to manifest his life's desires and create his own future as per his wishes while utilizing Samhara krama to dissolve and eventually destroy all karmic bonds. This balance of the two kramas helps the practitioner gain temporal and material benefits while also ensuring spiritual gains.

Swami Veda Bharati explains creation and dissolution thus: "Expansion and contraction in space are identical processes, just as creativity and entropy are interwoven. The boundaries between evolution and devolution cannot be determined. They are two sides of the same coin. This expansion and contraction are not opposite principles. They are not to be studied or even thought of in sequence. Evolution is devolution. Creation is dissolution. Creativity is entropy. The beginning is the end of any loop. And the universe is nothing if not a loop. There is nothing in the universe that is not a loop, a chakra, where one does not return to its origins."

In the Rig Veda, Sri Vidya is found as Sri Suktam. While in the Brahmanda Purana there is a comprehensive description of Sri Vidya, its method, and philosophy, it also finds mention in the Bhavanopanishad, Shiva Sutras, and Sri Vijjana Bhairava. The Bhavanopanishad is a major Sri Vidya text that postulates the symbolism of the Sri Chakra and outlines how this yantra is to be worshipped. The Saundarya Lahiri, composed by Adi Shankaracharya, is a hymn consisting of one hundred verses expounding the virtues of Lalitha Tripurasundari. It is considered the most beautiful and profound explanation of Sri Vidya and the Lalita Sahasranama, a very auspicious prayer containing one thousand names of the Devi is found in the Brahmanda Purana in the form of a discussion between Hayagreeva and sage Agasthya.

It is said that Brahma, Vishnu, Shiva, and the seven great rishis (Saptarishis) of the Hindu tradition have all been Sri Vidya Upasakas. Adi Shankaracharya was the greatest exponent of Sri Vidya and was instrumental in spreading this knowledge across India. Bhaskararaya, a renowned spiritual scholar who later took up sannyasa, was one of the foremost promoters of Sri Vidya in the 18th century. Sri Ramakrishna Paramahamsa and Swami Vivekananda are also known to be Sri Vidya Upasakas, who helped lend credibility and greater awareness to this school of worship. In modern times, Swami Amritananda and his disciple Raja Choudhury, Om Swami, Swami Karunamaya, and Sri M have been exponents of Sri Vidya.

Swami Veda Bharati writes that "Sri Vidya begins where the current understanding of quantum physics ends. It is the science of sciences, the mega-science, and the art of arts, the mega-art. Wherever we study configurations, charts, and graphs, it is a part of Sri Vidya. Wherever we study forms as fields of energy, it is Sri Vidya. Wherever we study Marmas in Ayurveda, this too is a part of Sri Vidya. But it is experienced only in the assimilation of these principles into our consciousness, not in an intellectual process but in our very being, in our very essence, so that our essence is not seen apart from the ever-expanding and contracting universe."

The Dasa Mahavidya is closely associated with the chakras, the energy centres that correspond to different aspects of consciousness and the physical body. Each of the ten Mahavidya is associated with a specific chakra, and the activation of that chakra can help connect the practitioner with the energy of the corresponding goddess. All the energies, except Bhairavi, are related to the higher chakras, pointing to their functions in the higher realms of consciousness as opposed to the lower, material realms.

1. Kali is associated with the Anahata (heart chakra) and all aspects of blood, including its production, circulation, etc.

2. Tara is related to both the Manipura (solar plexus chakra), where speech is first created as a thought form, and the Ajna (third eye chakra), where it is expressed as the uttered word.

3. Lalita Tripura Sundari sits at the Sahasrara (crown chakra).

4. Bhuvaneshwari is also associated with the Anahata (heart chakra), and according to the Katha Upanishad, she resides in the hridaya guha (the cave within which the osul resides).

5. Chhinnamasta controls Ajna (third eye chakra) and is involved in the upward movement of prana.

6. Bhairavi resides in the Muladhara (root chakra) in the form of Kundalini.

7. Dhumavati resides in the Anahata (heart chakra), where negative thoughts, painful memories, and past trauma are all stored.

8. Bagalamukhi sits in the upper palate at the relatively unknown Lalana chakra, connecting the tongue to the Ajna chakra.

9. Matangi presides over the Vishudda (throat chakra) as she controls speech.

10. Kamalatmika pervades the Anahata (heart chakra), governing experiences, allowing beauty and grace to nourish and nurture.

Tantric texts describe the Dasa Mahavidya energies that are present in the body as the ten types of prana, or life forces.

1. Prana Vayu, which is responsible for the intake of breath and governs the functions of the chest, heart, and respiratory system. It is associated with inhalation, energy absorption, and the movement of air. This prana is associated with Lalita Tripura Sundari.

2. Apana Vayu controls the downward and outward flow of energy in the body. It is responsible for elimination, including the functions of excretion, urination, menstruation, and childbirth. This prana is associated with Kali.

3. Samana Vayu is involved in the assimilation and digestion of food. It governs the movement of energy in the abdominal region, including the stomach and small intestines. This prana is associated with Dhumavati.

4. Udana Vayu is responsible for the upward movement of energy and controls speech, growth, and development. It governs functions such as swallowing, belching, and the movement of the diaphragm. This prana is associated with Bhairavi.

5. Vyana Vayu is responsible for the circulation of energy throughout the body. It governs the movements of the limbs, blood circulation, and sensory perceptions. This prana is associated with Matangi.

6. Naga vayu is associated with burping, eructation, and the expulsion of gas. It helps in the release of excess air from the stomach and aids in digestion. This prana is associated with Bhuvaneshwari.

7. Kurma Vayu governs the movements of the eyelids and is responsible for blinking. It protects the eyes and keeps them moist. This prana is associated with Tara.

8. Krikara Vayu controls the movement of the jaw and the opening and closing of the mouth. It aids in chewing and swallowing. This prana is associated with Bagalamukhi.

9. Devadatta Vayu is associated with yawning and is responsible for deep inhalations and exhalations. It helps regulate body temperature and relieve stress. This prana is associated with Chhinnamasta.

10. Dhananjaya Vayu governs the movement of the body after death. It is responsible for the decomposition of the body and the return of its elements to nature. This prana is associated with Kamalatmika.

The worship of specific deities of the Mahavidya is prescribed as an astrological remedy in Vedic Jyotishya. The Navagrahas are associated with different goddesses, while lagna is related to Bhairavi. The Navagrahas are the nine celestial bodies that are believed to have a significant influence on human lives and destinies. These celestial bodies are considered both deities and powerful cosmic forces that govern various aspects of human existence.

Each of the Mahavidya is associated with a planet (while Bhairavi is linked to the lagna), and any doshas or malefic effects of the planets can be countered by worshipping the specific deity linked to the planet. For example, if Saturn is in a house where it can cause difficulties, Kali, the governing goddess of Saturn, can be propitiated to get immediate relief from the problems. Vedic Jyotishya experts can suggest the most appropriate methods of appeasing the various planets.

- Surya (the sun) is regarded as the most important of the Navagrahas. It represents the soul, willpower, vitality, and overall life force. It is governed by Matangi.

- Chandra (the moon) represents the mind, emotions, and intuition. It influences mental well-being and emotional stability. It is governed by Bhuvaneshwari.

- Mangala (Mars) represents energy, courage, and ambition. It influences actions, passions, and relationships. It is governed by Bagalamukhi.

- Budha (Mercury) governs intelligence, communication, and intellect. It influences learning, speech, and analytical abilities. It is governed by Lalita Tripura Sundari.

- Guru (Jupiter) represents wisdom, knowledge, and spirituality. It influences growth, prosperity, and luck. It is governed by Tara.

- Shukra (Venus) symbolizes beauty, love, romance, and creativity. It influences relationships, artistic pursuits, and material comforts. It is governed by Kamalatmika.

- Shani (Saturn) represents discipline, justice, and karmic consequences. It influences hardships, delays, and life lessons. It is governed by Kali.

- Rahu (the North Lunar Node) is associated with worldly desires, ambition, and materialism. It influences careers, fame, and obsessions. It is governed by Chhinnamasta.

- Ketu (South Lunar Node) signifies spirituality, detachment, and liberation. It influences inner growth, intuition, and past-life connections. It is governed by Dhumavati.

- The Lagna is ascendant, the degree of the sign (rashi) that is rising on the eastern horizon at the time of one's birth. Bhairavi is in charge of Lagna.

The purpose of each Goddess, through their physical characteristics and unique attributes, is to awaken some sentiment or feeling that lies deep within our subconscious. We all carry hidden desires, repressed memories, and unresolved trauma, which come to the fore when we hear these mythological stories that tell of different situations that can arise in life. We may find ourselves deeply attracted to one particular story, resonating with its implied truths. We may find ourselves feeling an aversion to some of the energy forms. Both are natural and help us understand something about our own psychology, which we can then start to explore further and initiate the process of healing and moving forward. Perhaps we can draw a parallel with the Freudian request to come forward with our pain, accept that we are products of our experiences, and welcome catharsis. As John Woodroffe said: "We are now illuminated by Her light, now wrapped in her terrible darkness.' The dark beauty of Kali, creatrix of worlds, transcends us all.

As we have traversed the entire spectrum of divinity, from the fierce energies of the Ugra manifestations to the grace-giving and benevolent energies of the Soumya forms, we are reminded of Krishna's words in the Bhagavat Gita:

Ye yatha mam prapadyante, tan tathaiva bhajami aham

I appear to my devotees in the way that they seek me

The Mahavidya too are one, but they appear to us in the form that we seek and relate to the most. It is the same Shakti who created the universe, and she can assume any form or shape and appear anywhere and everywhere, all at once. The Dasa Mahavidya are profound and transformative archetypes, providing a framework for understanding and engaging with the diverse aspects of the Divine Feminine. Their worship and practices engage practitioners on multiple levels, fostering holistic growth and integration and acting as a catalyst for holistic transformation and spiritual empowerment in all aspects of life.

Sri Matrye Namah

References

1. Charles Mackenzie: The Devī Gītā: The Song of the Goddess

2. Shankarnarayanan. S: The Ten Great Cosmic Powers: Dasa Mahavidyas

3. Daniélou, Alain :The Myths and Gods of India: The Classic Work on Hindu Polytheism

4. Kinsley, David R : Hindu Goddesses: Vision of the Divine Feminine in the Hindu Religious Tradition

5. J. Gordon Melton; Baumann, Martin: Religions of the World: A Comprehensive Encyclopedia of Beliefs and Practices

6. Sri Amritananda Natha Saraswati's works

7. Dr David Frawley: Tantric Yoga and the Wisdom Goddesses

8. Dr Sonja Lyubomirsky: Gratitude is Best Attitude (Mindforest)

9. P.R. Krishna Kumar: The Sri Chakra as a symbol of the human body

10. Lalithananda Lalita Prasad Jammulamadaka: Sri Vidya and Sri Chakra

11. Bernhard Wimmer: Sri Yantra

12. Sri Yantra Research Centre

13. Gerard Huet : Sri Yantra

14. Gaia: How to harness the power of Sri Yantra

15. Davidji: How to meditate with Sri Yantra

16. Madhu Khanna: Yantra, the tantric symbol of cosmic unity

17. Rohit Arya: Symbolism of the Sri Yantra

18. Dhyana Foundation: Sri Yantra

19. Sreenivasa Rao's blogs: Sri Chakra

20. Prof. S.K. Ramachandra Rao: The Tantra of Sri Chakra Bhavanopanishad

21. Subhash Kak: The great goddess Lalitha and the Sri Chakra

22. Sri Sivapremanandaji – Sri Vidya Sadhana

23. International Journal of Geology, Agriculture and Environmental Sciences, Vol 5 Issue 2

24. Swami Satyanand Saraswati: The Fantastic Science of Yantra

25. Devadatta Kali (Vedanta Society of California): The Mahavidyas

26. Avalon Arthur: Shakti and Shakta

27. S. Sankaranarayanan: Ten Great Cosmic Powers

28. Sri Amrita Ananda: Sri Devi Khadgamala

29. V Ravi: Understanding and Worshipping Sri Chakra

30. Hindupedia

31. Mircea Eliade: The Sacred and the Profane: The Nature of Religion: The Significance of Religious Myth, Symbolism, and Ritual within Life and Culture

32. Antonotea Gotea: Hridaya Yoga

33. From Britannica on topic of Karma

34. Maya Tiwari: The Path of Practice: A Woman's Book of Ayurvedic Healing

35. Dr. David Frawley: Yoga & Ayurveda, Self-Healing and Self-Realization

36. Judith Anodea: Wheels of Life

37. Judith Anodea: Eastern Body, Western Mind: Psychology and the Chakra System As a Path to the Self

38. Caroline Myss: Anatomy of the Spirit: The Seven Stages of Power and Healing

39. Tiffany Luptak: The Chakras: Inner Portals to Harmony

40. Felise Bermen: Swadhisthana the Second Chakra, one's own abode

41. Tantric Master Shri Aghorinath Ji: "A Tantric Masters View of Tantra."

42. Michael M Bowden: Gifts from the Goddess: Selected Works of Sri Amritananda Natha Saraswathi

43. Kavitha Chinnaiyan: Glorious Alchemy: Living the Lalita Sahasranama

44. Dr. Shashi Tharoor: The Hindu Way: An Introduction to Hinduism

Website URL

www. vedanta.org/2010/monthly-readings/the-mahavidyas-the-powers-of-consciousness-conceptualized-part-1/

www.exoticindiaart.com/article/mahavidyas/

www.hinduwebsite.com/hinduism/h_time.asp

www.shreemaa.org/story-of-origindas-mahavidyas/

ratiwrites.com/2019/06/19/dasa-mahavidya-the-ten-great-wisdoms/

manblunder.com/articles/dasa-mahavidya

www.indica.today/quick-reads/dasha-mahavidyas

www.hinduonline.co/vedicreserve/tantra/dasamahavidya.pdf

www.sivasakti.com/tantra/dasa-maha-vidya/god-in-ten-parts/

engelsbergideas.com/notebook/a-little-history-of-the-fierce-goddess/

vedanta.org/2014/monthly-readings/kali-retreat-led-by-david-nelson/

adishakti.org/subtle_system/mooladhara_chakra

drvidyahattangadi.com/water-has-memory/

www.psychologytoday.com/us/experts/ilene-strauss-cohen-phd

www.shivashantiyoga.com/the-second-chakra-swadistana-ones-own-abode/

kathycaprino/2018/11/28/three-simple-steps-to-identify-your-life-purpose-and-leverage-it-in-your-career

www.psychologytoday.com/us/blog/think-well/201802/how-respond-criticism

hbr.org/2011/04/strategies-for-learning-from-failure

www.calmwithyoga.com/get-more-mental-clarity-emotional-stability-well-being-by-activating-heart-coherence/

www.swami-krishnananda.org

theophilelancien.org/en/anahata-chakra-3-antelope-sy

daringtolivefully.com/spend-more-time-in-nature

thegoddessgarden.com/throat-chakra-vishuddha-chakra

roamingyogi.co/throat-chakra-vishuddha-chakra-fifth-chakra

www.yogajournal.com/yoga-101/chakratuneup2015-intro-visuddha

www.tantra-kundalini.com/vishuddha/

ancient.eu/shiva

www.adventureyogi.com/blog/chakra-series-vishuddha-chakra/

www.goodnet.org/articles/chakra-healing-how-to-open-your-throat

www.eternalhealthyoga.com/ehy/2018/12/05/vishuddha-chakra-say-say/

yogainternational.com/article/view/4-degrees-of-human-speech

callofthevedas.wordpress.com/2015/10/30/managing-taming-and-dissolving-anger/

tamilandvedas.com/tag/four-types-of-anger/

www.theguardian.com/lifeandstyle/2016/nov/25/how-to-be-a-good-listener-the-experts-guide

hbr.org/2016/07/what-great-listeners-actually-do

www.yogajournal.com/yoga-101/talk-pretty

www.nytimes.com/2017/05/08/smarter-living/why-you-should-learn-to-say-no-more-often

www.yogajournal.com/teach/yoga-and-samkhya-purifying-the-elements-of-the-human-being

www.-anatomy.com/third-eye-chakra.html

www.tantra-kundalini.com/ajna/

www.yogajournal.com/yoga-101/chakratuneup2015-intro-ajna

chopra.com/articles/trust-your-intuition-with-the-sixth-chakra

www.chakras.info/third-eye-chakra/

www.psychologytoday.com/intl/blog/the-intuitive-compass/201108/what-is-intuition-and-how-do-we-use-it

www.huffingtonpost.in/entry/the-habits-of-highly-intuitive-people

www.nei.nih.gov/learn-about-eye-health/healthy-vision/how-eyes-work

www.businessinsider.in/science/a-neuroscientist-explains-why-reality-may-just-be-a-hallucination

yogachicago.com/2014/01/om-the-sacred-pranava-everything-you-wanted-to-know-about-

www.pranava.com/pranava_whatis.html

letitgoyoga.com/indigo-is-the-color-of-the-sixth-chakra

lonerwolf.com/third-eye-chakra-healing/

www.chakras.info/crown-chakra/

www.yogiapproved.com/om/the-crown-chakra-how-it-connects-you-to-the-Divine/

lonerwolf.com/crown-chakra-healing/

powerthoughtsmeditationclub.com/the-chakras/

www.yogapedia.com/definition/5370/vairagya

www.esamskriti.com/e/Spirituality/Philosophy/What-is-VAIRAGYA-1.aspx

ausram.blogspot.com/2014/01/an-amazing-verse-from-bhagavad-gita.html

www.speakingtree.in/blog/sadhana-chatushtaya-varanana

www.yogapedia.com/definition/10768/sadhana-chatushtaya

zenhabits.net/simple-living-manifesto-72-ideas-to-simplify-your-life/

medium.com/@zamirdhanji/when-the-student-is-ready-the-master-appears

tayyoga.wordpress.com/2017/12/27/part-16-koshas-and-chakras/

www.amcollege.edu/blog/balancing-chakras

greatergood.berkeley.edu/article/item/how_modern_life_became_disconnected_from_nature

www.learnreligions.com/what-is-tantra-1770612

www.yogajournal.com/philosophy/tantra-rising/

Kanakadhara Stotram – http://Divine-Thought.blogspot.com/

ramanisblog.in/2017/07/16/perfect-sri-chakra-by-adi-shankaracharya-sringeri/

www.newstatesman.com/blogs/the-faith-column

https://en.wikipedia.org/wiki/Tantra

matthiasrose.medium.com/the-origins-of-tantra-acc4334638e9

www.shankaracharya.org/soundarya_lahari.php

www.kamakotimandali.com/srividya/urahasya.html

www.fearlessculture.design/blog-posts/the-power-of-rituals-how-to-build-meaningful-habits

www.sonima.com/yoga/sanskrit-mantras/

www.yogamag.net/archives/1970s/1978/isep78/pm978.html

www.claritychi.com/the-importance-of-rituals/

jamesmchapman.com/2014/12/01/the-vritti-samskara-chakra/

www.sivanandaonline.org/

www.yogabasics.com/learn/the-five-vayus

jamesmchapman.com/2014/12/01/the-vritti-samskara-chakra/

www.yogabasics.com/connect/yoga-blog/samskaras-unraveling-the-conditioned-self/

www.facebook.com/notes/hindu-dharmika-sansthan/mantra-vidya

www.vedanet.com/mantra-concentration-and-meditation/

www.sivasakti.com/tantra/introduction-to-yantra/yantras-dasha-maha-vidyas/

mmpandit.wordpress.com/2015/06/23/the-devatas-of-aghora-and-tantra-the-great-widow/

swarajyamag.com/culture/fierce-is-beautiful

www.encyclopedia.com/environment/encyclopedias-almanacs-transcripts-and-maps/goddess-worship-hindu-goddess

www.exoticindiaart.com/book/details/sakti-s-revolution-origins-and-historiography-of-indic-fierce-goddesses-naf053/

www.qz.com/1768545/hinduisms-kali-is-the-feminist-icon-the-world-desperately-needs

Also by this author

Sri Chakra Yantra

Manifest anything with the symbol of everything

Discover how a 12,000-year-old mystical symbol holds the key to awakening your deepest inner potential and enhancing your powers of manifestation.

The Sri Chakra Yantra is an ancient symbol depicting the process of creation in a powerful matrix which represents the macrocosm (the Universe) and microcosm (the human body), thus acting as a powerful, cosmic antenna that allows you direct access to communicate with the Universe.

The book delves into some metaphysical aspects which are reflected in the philosophies underlying Shaktism, Tantra, Dasa Mahavidya and Sri Vidya. Once these concepts throw some light on the basis of Sri Chakra worship, the nature of sacred geometry and the significance, structure and meaning of the Sri Chakra Yantra is explained. This is followed by chapters that focus on the relationship of the human body to the Sri Chakra and its connection with the Pineal Gland. There is also a brief note on healing and the Sri Chakra.

The use of sounds in the path to spiritual growth is discussed with a special focus on the sounds (mantras and stotras) associated with the Sri Chakra Yantra. The book describes the role of mudras and contains details about the initial infusion of energy into the yantra, the method of worship, the path to visualisation and meditation on the Sri Chakra.

Also by this author

Chakras

Learn all about the Chakras - mystical energy centres that are integral to the ancient Indian traditions of Yoga and Ayurveda. The Chakras are inner portals of harmony, linking the physical and spiritual planes, offering a deep and time-tested formula for transformation, abundance and the ability to hack into one's power of manifestation.

This book equips you using simple, everyday language to harness the potential of the tremendous internal energy pools that lie dormant in the body and help you channel it and act upon your life purpose by presenting Chakras as a tool for self-development. The book delves into concepts such as Sankhya, Yoga philosophies and the Karma doctrine in order to establish the context of how the Chakra energies work.

The author has kept in mind the sensibilities of the modern spiritual seeker and their needs and interests, presenting the information in a non-dogmatic and practical manner, thereby allowing everyone an opportunity to learn and experience the benefits of awakening the Chakra energies.

Also by this author

Tantra Mantra and Yantra of Sri Vidya

"Sri Vidya begins where the current understanding of quantum physics ends", say modern-day scholars about this little-known, highly esoteric spiritual tradition that has been carefully kept under wraps by its secretive and serious practitioners. The study of Sri Vidya is fascinating as much as it is frustrating because information about its various aspects is tough to find. This book is an endeavour to explore the Sri Vidya tradition and understand it as the unfolding of Shakti, the inherent power which lies at the core of our being and holds the key to our worldly and spiritual success.

Sri Vidya practice comprises tantra (a technique or framework for worship) whose two main elements are mantra (sacred sound) and yantra (sacred geometry). Tantra can be described in simple terms as the utilisation of the mental faculty to pursue the objectives of worship using mantra and yantra. Mantra is the use of sound energy to bring about oneness with the Divine, while yantra is a geometric drawing which serves as a tool to reach the Divine.

The book delves into concepts such as Sankhya, Yoga, Karma and Kundalini in order to establish the context of how Sri Vidya is to be approached, combining elements of knowledge, devotion and ritual.

The author has kept in mind the sensibilities of the modern spiritual seeker and their needs and interests, presenting the information in a non-dogmatic and practical manner, thereby allowing everyone an opportunity to learn and experience the benefits of Sri Vidya.

This is the third book by the author in the Spirituality Series. The first book was about the Sri Chakra Yantra and the second book had Chakras as its subject.

Also by this author

The Sacred Sounds of Sri Vidya

We find the term "anavritti shabdat" in the Vedanta Sutra. This concept can be understood as utilising the power of sound to attain liberation. Mantras, potent sound forms passed on from generations, not only have the power to evoke positivity but can transform the reality of our perception by bringing about a heightened state of awareness. The Sri Vidya tradition is rich in mantras dedicated to defining the glory of Shakti. This book is an endeavour to explore the main mantras used in the Sri Vidya tradition and understand them as the unfolding of Shakti, the inherent power which lies at the core of our being and holds the key to our worldly and spiritual success.

"Sri Vidya begins where the current understanding of quantum physics ends", say modern-day scholars about this little known, highly esoteric spiritual tradition that has been carefully kept under wraps by its practitioners. Sri Vidya practise is a three-fold one, encompassing mantra (sacred sound), yantra (sacred geometry) and tantra (a technique or framework for worship). Learning about the mantras used in the Sri Vidya tradition is fascinating as it spans an array of techniques, texts and philosophical concepts.

Our minds and beliefs can be our strongest allies or our worst enemies. The book delves into concepts such as the importance of building the right narrative about life and the need for ritual in modern-day lifestyle. Samskara, vritti and vasana are described along with a detailed study of tantra and Sri Vidya before a discussion on mantras in general and then focussing on the mantras used in the Sri Vidya tradition. The subjects covered seek to establish the context of mantra sadhana in Sri Vidya is to be approached, combining elements of knowledge, devotion and ritual.